THE SENIOR DRIVER'S GUIDEBOOK

HOW TO KEEP DRIVING LONGER

AND

SURVIVE IN THE 21ST CENTURY

KEN D. SMITH

Five Star Publishing
A Division of Matthew J. Key & Associates, Inc.
Stillwater, Minnesota

THE SENIOR DRIVER'S GUIDEBOOK
HOW TO KEEP DRIVING LONGER AND SURVIVE IN THE 21st CENTURY

For information write: Five Star Publishing, (A Division of Matthew J. Key & Associates, Inc.) P. O. Box 4, Stillwater, Minnesota 55082-4298

Editors: Matthew J. Key & Linda J. Wells

First Edition

Manufactured in the United States of America

Published by: Five Star Publishing

Clipart by Microsoft® Word 97 SR-1

Printed by: Banta Information Services Group - Eden Prairie, Minnesota

Publisher's Cataloging-in-Publication
(Provided by Quality Books, Inc.)

Smith, Ken, 1921-
  The senior driver's guidebook : how to keep driving longer and survive in the 21st century / Ken Smith. -- 1st ed.
  p. cm.
  Includes bibliographical references and index.
  LCCN: 98-93920
  ISBN: 0-9617996-1-7
  1. Automobile driving. 2. Aged automobile drivers.
I. Title.
TL152.5.S65 1999   629.28'3
           QBI99-745

ACKNOWLEDGMENTS

It would not have occurred to me to write this guidebook if I had not reached the stage in life where I observed drivers my own age making terrible mistakes. This observation caused me to realize that I would be remiss if I did not pass on some of my experience and knowledge.

The writing of this book would have been impossible without the generous help of many individuals. Thank you all for your assistance and encouragement. Special thanks go to Jean Hanson - Manager, Quality & Risk, Health Span Transportation Services, Mike Mahoney - Publisher, Stillwater Evening Gazette Newspaper, Richard Morel - President & Training Consultant, R.J. Morel & Associates, Pat Bell - Midwest Independent Publisher's Association, and Tom Langford - WEZU-AM Radio, Stillwater, Minnesota, and Dan Poynter - Author & Publisher, Para Publishing, for their contributions and valuable advice.

Thank you Matt Key, for showing me the way and providing knowledge of the mechanics of putting a book together.

It seems too that this writing has become a family venture with excellent suggestions and encouragement from my daughter, Susan Clasen. They were appreciated. My granddaughter, Tina Clasen, provided computer expertise and advice which helped to pull it all together. Thank you, Tina. Thank you to my loyal wife and friend, Mary, without whose encouragement I would never have started the book. She was a faithful reader and helped me stay on course to complete it.

Finally, I am especially indebted and grateful to my daughter, Linda Wells, who spent untold hours at her computer, composing, editing, and processing the manuscript and providing invaluable assistance.

Disclaimer

The Senior Driver's Guidebook was written to provide mature drivers with up-to-date and pertinent information to ensure safe driving survival into the 21st Century.

The guidebook does not claim to cover every aspect of driving safety, as this could not be covered in a single publication. This book is only a guide and is not intended to take the place of a driver examination, road test, or certified driver education program. It does, however, go beyond other manuals of this type by detailing specific crash prevention techniques for senior drivers.

The author and Five Star Publishing shall have neither liability nor responsibility to any person or entity with respect to any loss or damage caused, or alleged to have been caused, directly or indirectly by the information contained in this book.

Contents

Contents

Introduction

This book ***"THE SENIOR DRIVER'S GUIDEBOOK - HOW TO KEEP DRIVING LONGER AND SURVIVE IN THE 21st CENTURY"*** has been written to help ensure that experienced mature drivers, will continue to survive on today's "pressure cooker" roadways.

Grim statistics on all levels, national, state and local, show that every few minutes a driver, passenger, or pedestrian is killed or injured in a vehicle crash with economic losses costing billions nationwide. It is not possible to access how much monetary loss is suffered by surviving families, let alone losses to the community.

We feel that defensive driving and an awareness of the factors causing crashes can eliminate a large number of these crashes and subsequent losses. Crowded roadways coupled with today's aggressive drivers call for special measures. So we have detailed and outlined hundreds of proven ways that senior drivers can be better, smarter and safer drivers.

In a world where the driving environment is constantly changing and the senior driver is looked upon by some as a menace on the roadway, we who have reached the "mature driver" stage need an honest self-evaluation. We need an update to our knowledge, and a review of safety techniques required for us to stay alive while driving. This "how to" guide will provide the framework for developing the improved skills needed to cope with the changing traffic scene.

Senior driver performance regularly becomes a "front burner" issue at legislative sessions. Many legislative constituents propose various senior issues. Among those issues is the requirement that after a certain age seniors be required to pass a stringent test before driver license renewal. I foresee the time when all seniors will be required to take and pass a road test. Many, as a result of that testing, will be granted the privilege to drive but will have a restricted license and will only be allowed to drive to the bank, a store, and their church. Further, they will not be allowed to drive on any freeway, drive at night or during rush hour and/or only within 25 miles of their residence.

While we feel road testing for seniors would be a good thing, we feel the driving public would be better served if **all drivers** were required to pass a periodic road test. It must be noted that unqualified and even impaired drivers come from **every age group!**

The driving safety of all of us depends to a large extent on driving attitudes and skills of ALL drivers. With the daily demonstrations of wildly aggressive and impulsive drivers on our roadways it is quite obvious that consideration and basic courtesy seems to have been forgotten. "Look out for me, get out of my way," seems to be what a lot of drivers are saying, while many refuse to accept responsibility for their own actions. Bad attitudes and bad driving have taken over our roadways, and are why you will see how important **defensive driving** has become to those of us who want to survive.

We are proud to present this comprehensive senior driver's guide with a "Before You Drive" checklist, and hundreds of safe driving tips. This guide provides proven driving strategies and is a refresher course to improve your driving performance, extend your driving independence, and help pass any test you may be required to take.

Our driving ability and everyday skill will be the measure of how we survive the changing and oftentimes dangerous driving environment of the 21st century.

Chapter One

THE SENIOR DRIVER

Some Key Points in this Chapter

- Does chronological age really measure our abilities?

- Does driving self-regulation work?

- Can senior drivers be better drivers?

- Crash Facts and Performance Records.

- Is age the sole indicator of driving ability?

- Why use the term "crash" instead of "accident"?

- Can seniors improve their driving skills?

Chapter One

THE SENIOR DRIVER

Senior Driving Problems

Most senior drivers resent being called part of a "senior driving problem." In fact, they many times see younger drivers as the real hazard on the road, and cite statistics that fortify their belief.

As seniors age, abilities may clash with safety. However, driving is not only important to us, but also to the economy. None of us wants to give up the independence that driving our own vehicle gives us. Even though our eyesight is not what it once was, we may not able to hear as well as we would like, and we may not have the mobility we once had, we are reluctant to give up driving. We feel that seniors should not have to give up driving until our performance reaches the point where our diminished capacity inevitably forces us to exit the road. We can, however, put off hanging up our car keys. There are many things we can do now to bring our driving up to a higher standard in order to keep driving longer.

Research by the National Institute on Aging has found that:
1. Our chronological age alone does not accurately measure our functional abilities;
2. Senior drivers' capabilities, knowledge and ability to function safely *vary within the same age group;* and
3. Older "problem drivers" are usually those that deny that their skills are worsening even as they function less safely.

The same researchers have found that for most seniors, driving skills actually do decline with age. This decline can start as early as age 55, and by age 75 has dropped dramatically. Is there anything positive at all in this picture? Yes, most definitely! As they age, senior drivers tend to *self-regulate* themselves in many ways. They may avoid high-risk rush hour freeway traffic, may stay off roadways during periods of inclement weather, and avoid nighttime driving. These are all good choices.

In 1900, only 4% of Americans were 65 years of age or older. In 1988, 12% were 65 or older. By 2020, there will be an estimated 17% or 50 million persons over the age of 65. Researchers estimate that there are 6000 persons joining the ranks every day, and many will still be eligible to drive by that year. We hope they do and, in fact, the national economy depends on this group of people. As consumers they are a very important part of the nation's economic health, and their "getting around" is vital to the economy.

We think it is questionable that the driving environment will improve in the next century. So the question remains, does the experience and maturity of older drivers make them better drivers compared to drivers in other age groups?

As the facts show, **there are problem drivers in every group**. So we may wonder whether senior drivers can be better drivers in spite of their age limitations? The information presented in **How To Keep Driving Longer And Survive in the 21st Century** will provide the answers and the "know how" that will help each senior driver answer the question in the affirmative!

SENIOR CRASH FACTS

Driver Licensing Administrators maintain that by the year 2020, traffic deaths of those 65 years of age and older will increase by 50% over the present. Those are shocking figures! Older, however, does have its advantages. While the tolerance to injury reduces as we age, the risk of involvement in a fatal crash declines until about age 75.

Fact: Crash data indicates that in many ways older drivers are more cautious, even more sensible than some other driving groups.

Fact: Unskilled, impaired or unqualified drivers come from **all** age groups.

Fact: Older drivers are oftentimes spotlighted as the ones causing a collision, due to widespread prejudice against senior drivers.

Fact: Research indicates that with increased age comes an accompanying weakening of physical ability, along with slower reaction time.

Fact: Senior drivers are found to be involved in a disproportionately high percentage of motor vehicle crashes based on the number of vehicle miles driven, with a much higher crash rate for drivers 70 years of age and over. Drivers over age 85 have 2½ times as many crashes as average.

The National Highway Transportation Safety Administration (NHTSA) has found that in crashes nationwide, **the older driver is at fault more frequently than middle aged drivers**. This kind of data, coupled with publicized crash coverage by media of crashes alleged to be the fault of senior drivers, has caused some people to propose that drivers over the age of 60-65 should be required to take a driver license examination before each application for license renewal. While there is really no solid statistical basis for such action, it will most likely not be long before passing a written examination and road test will become mandatory for seniors to retain their driving privileges.

Fact: Researchers have found that a person's age should not be the criteria for determining whether or not he or she should be licensed.

Fact: Currently, injuries due to car crashes are the leading cause of accidental death of drivers ages 65-75 and of half of those over the age of 75. For all drivers over the age of 65, crashes are 3.5 times more likely to be fatal. Part of this startling crash fact is due to their greater vulnerability to injury. *Minnesota Motor Vehicle Crash Facts.*

Perhaps you may have noticed that we do not use the term "accident." Why? The concept of "accident" implies that drivers were unable to use corrective or preventable actions and that the safe operation of a motor vehicle is really **outside human influence**. Using "accident", rather than "crash" or "collision" also fosters the idea that damages, injuries and fatalities in a motor vehicle collision are **unavoidable**. Our years of experience in the driver safety field has convinced us that **every driver can learn and should take action to alter their driving skills in order to avoid vehicle collisions or crashes**.

The Senior Drivers Guidebook will address some of the problems that contribute to the crash record, and make suggestions as to how we as a group can eliminate old "bad habits" to improve our driving. These things will enable us to more easily pass any test required of us in the future. The ultimate result, and most beneficial one, will be our extended longevity as **safer senior drivers**.

WHAT HAVE I LEARNED?

TRUE OR FALSE?

1. If we make an honest evaluation of our driving habits and make some changes we can "avoid hanging up our car keys".
2. Our chronological age is an accurate measure of how well we function as a driver.
3. Senior drivers capabilities seldom vary within the age group.
4. Driving skills really don't start declining until about age 70.
5. Unskilled, impaired and even unqualified drivers come from ALL age groups.
6. The senior driver is at fault in auto crashes more frequently than middle aged drivers.
7. Proposals are being made nationwide to require driver testing of drivers above 60-65.
8. Use of the term "accident" implies that drivers are not able to use preventable actions to avoid vehicle collisions.

ANSWERS:

1. True
2. False
3. False
4. False
5. True
6. True
7. True
8. True

Chapter Two

HOW DOES AGE AFFECT OUR DRIVING

Some Key Points in this Chapter

- Have we on occasion missed a sign or signal?

- Are highway and/or freeway driving getting difficult?

- Have you received a traffic citation recently?

- Rate Yourself - A "Before You Drive" Checklist.

- Checklist answers and Safe Driving Tips.

- Are we slowing down in spite of ourselves?

- What are some compensating strategies?

Chapter Two

HOW DOES AGE AFFECT OUR DRIVING?

RATE YOURSELF: A "BEFORE YOU DRIVE" CHECKLIST

Indicate Yes or No

_____ 1. Have you on occasion missed a sign or signal?

_____ 2. Are other drivers in too big of a rush?

_____ 3. Are gaps in traffic harder to judge?

_____ 4. Roads are getting confusing or I sometimes get lost?

_____ 5. Cars suddenly come from nowhere?

_____ 6. Do you take any medicine that may impair your driving?

_____ 7. Is it getting difficult to make a sharp turn?

_____ 8. Do drivers seem to stop suddenly in front of you?

_____ 9. Is highway and freeway driving getting to be difficult?

_____ 10. Night driving is sometimes hard to cope with.

_____ 11. I always wear my seat belt.

_____ 12. I lose my temper at some traffic situations.

_____ 13. I shy away from turning left at some intersections.

_____ 14. Usually I drive with one foot on the brake and one on the gas.

_____ 15. I always use my turn signal when turning, changing lanes and driving away from the curb.

_____ 16. Have you gotten a citation for a moving violation or a warning from a traffic officer ?

_____ 17. I have had more than one minor vehicle crash during the past two years.

_____ 18. I often watch scenery and talk to others while driving.

CHECKLIST ANSWERS and SAFE DRIVING TIPS

"Self awareness is critical to your driving safety"

1. **Have you on occasion missed a sign or signal?**
   Your answer should have been **No**.
   Safe Driving Tip: Make sure you know all signs by their shape and know the standard symbols. Scan the roadway for signals and drive familiar routes.

2. **Are other drivers in too big a rush?**
   Safe Driving Tip: Drive the speed limit, if practical. Drive in the right hand lane, especially on freeways. Do not drive too slowly. This is as unsafe as driving too fast!

3. **Are gaps in traffic harder to judge? Are you finding it difficult to join freeway traffic?**
   Safe Driving Tip: Do not feel pressured into making a turn or entering a traffic controlled intersection until you are sure you can do it safely. If you have stopped using the freeway then by all means take a refresher course or ask another experienced driver to ride with you and practice when traffic is less congested.

4. **Roads are sometimes getting confusing or I get lost.**
   Safe Driving Tip: Drive during non-rush hours whenever possible. Think ahead and plan your routes on familiar roads.

5. **Do cars suddenly come from nowhere?**
   Safe Driving Tip: Be alert! Look out for other cars. Please do not stare straight ahead while driving. Make sure mirrors are adjusted and adequate and then use them. Scan the road for other cars and concentrate on the traffic around you.

6. **Do you take any medicine that may impair your driving?**
   Safe Driving Tip: Ask your doctor or pharmacist if your prescription will affect your driving.

7. **Is it getting difficult to make sharp turns ?**
   Safe Driving Tip: If necessary, slow down to stay in your lane while turning. Always use your turn signal and be sure it has canceled after completing your turn.

8. **Do drivers seem to stop suddenly in front of you ?**
Safe Driving Tip: Keep *one car length* between you and the car in front of you for each 10 mph of speed you are traveling . . . that is *minimum*. A better rule is the "two second rule." To use, pick a fixed reference point at the side of the road ahead, such as a telephone pole, post or bridge. Watch the car in front when it passes this point. Then count, "One-Thousand-One, One-Thousand-Two." If you pass the reference point *before* you are through counting, you are following too closely. Keep a safe distance between your vehicle and the vehicle in front of you.

9. **Are highway and/or freeway driving getting to be difficult?**
Safe Driving Tip: Stay in the lane traveling closest to your speed. The right lane is preferable at all times. The left lane is for those who usually do not drive the speed limit. Congested traffic situations should be avoided.

10. **Night driving is sometimes hard to cope with.**
Safe Driving Tip: Look away from headlight glare. As a vehicle approaches you with their headlights on look at the side white line on the right side of the road. Keep your headlight lenses clean. Try to use roads you are familiar with. If it is still difficult, limit night driving.

11. **I always wear my seat belt.**
Safe Driving Tip: 50% of all traffic fatalities would have been injury-only crashes if those involved had been wearing the 3-point seat belts. *Remember*, if you are a senior you are more likely to be injured or killed than a driver under the age of 55 is.

These are very valid reasons why you should be wearing your seat belt at all times, and *convince your passengers* that you mean it when you say, "This car will not start unless everyone is buckled up." Some states make it illegal to operate your vehicle unless the front right seat passenger is buckled up also.

12. **I lose my temper at some traffic situations.**
Safe Driving Tip: Anger behind the wheel comes out in dangerous ways. Some are calling it "road rage." If you find you have driven too closely behind someone to "teach him or her a lesson," ask yourself, "what did I accomplish? Was it worth it?" Accept the fact that you *cannot be a traffic judge while on the road*. Relax and be responsible.

13. **I shy away from turning left at some intersections.**

    Safe Driving Tip: Intersections are the most common place for vehicle crashes. Plan your trips to avoid those that give you trouble. Plan alternate routes. Remember, going beyond that intersection one block and turning right three times will solve that problem.

14. **Usually I drive with one foot on the brake and one on the gas pedal.**

    Safe Driving Tip: This bad habit will get you in a lot of trouble. It can quickly result in loss of car control, and you will fail the road test if your friendly Driver Examiner catches you at it. Safety experts tell you no, but your brake repairman loves you for doing it. Remember, you are signaling to those driving behind you that you are stopping when actually you are not. How confusing!

15. **I always use turn signals when turning, changing lanes and driving away from the curb.**

    Safe Driving Tip: This is one habit everyone should have. Why have to think, "shall I signal now?" If you are only using your signals "part time," correct that bad habit now. Using only your mirrors will not do. Driver Examiners expect you to look over your shoulder for every move.

16. **Have you gotten a citation for a moving violation or a warning from a traffic officer ?**

    Safe Driving Tip: If you answered "yes," perhaps this was not the "minor" thing that you would like to think it was. Determine at once to read Chapters Three and Five carefully and make notes. Chapter Six will expose some driving problems and provide solutions.

17. **I have had more than one minor vehicle crash during the past two years.**

    Safe Driving Tip: You are probably more than likely to be involved in a vehicle crash again. Just being involved, **_regardless of fault_**, is usually an indicator of some future crash. We have to work harder than younger drivers to react properly and quickly to sudden potential crash situations. Do you know what they are? Many of them will be covered later in this guidebook. See Chapter Six for more information on this subject.

18. **I often watch scenery and talk to others while driving.**

Safe Driving Tip: It is a good idea to eliminate distractions and keep sightseeing to a minimum. It is better to find a safe place to pull over and stop to enjoy the view. Taking your eyes off the road for even one moment can be deadly. Looking for an address? Again, stop your vehicle where safe and survey the area before proceeding.

Most of us have a difficult time dealing with distractions, especially when traffic is congested. We need more information and more time to decide what we are going to do in certain situations. We may have to ask our passengers to limit their conversation until we drive out of the area we are in. Some who are not drivers may not understand, but as the driver it is your responsibility to make sure you all arrive at your destination safely.

Most all your answers to the checklist should have been **no**. Your answers give you an indication of your present understanding. Your answers may either confirm what you already know, or improve your driving knowledge.

Also, you no doubt have even found some *"reminders"* or *new* Safety Driving Tips that can help compensate for those age-related changes and bad habits that affect all of us.

Senior Drivers can be better drivers !

SLOWING DOWN? SOME TELL-TALE SIGNS

By the year 2000, 1 of every 3 drivers in America will be over 55 years of age. Our freedom to drive will be an important factor in maintaining our personal freedom and mental health.

Remember when we first began to drive? Two lane roads, very few traffic signs, manual transmissions, no outside mirrors, no power equipment, no standardized traffic laws or signs. ***Driving for us back at that time was easy***. However, age does influence our ability to function in traffic with the same ease that we had when we were in our twenties and thirties. Our age has forced us to modify our driving behavior and some of us have cut back drastically on our driving. Let's admit it, most of us are slowing down in spite of ourselves.

What are some of the telltale signs?
1. Are we having difficulty distinguishing between colors?
2. Is the guy behind us sounding his horn more frequently when the traffic light changes to green?
3. Have you ever found yourself slowing or even stopping at an intersection when the light is green?
4. Are we finding that we are having frequent "fender bender" type crashes?
5. Have we backed into another car or post at the mall without realizing it?
6. How is our knowledge of traffic signs ? One recent study found that when tested on the meanings of a sign, "almost all seniors failed to understand at least one device." *National Safety Council (NSC) - Traffic Safety Magazine.*

These are just a few of the "**signals.**" If you recognize some of these tell tale signs in your own driving, or have found that some of your answers to the "Before You Drive" checklist did not agree with ours, take the time now to make some changes.

The normal age-related physical changes that affect our driving ability may sneak up on us, but we do not have to let them force us out of the driver's seat. A recent study found that some drivers over the age of 65 voluntarily gave up driving, due to the fact they were the first to recognize the tell tale signs of slowing down and felt they were at risk to themselves and others.

Another study found that some senior drivers recognize the driving hazards and cope by adopting some strategies to compensate. They are:

1. Exercising greater caution by changing automobile usage, including shorter trips and driving in off-peak hours.

2. Avoidance of unpredictable and uncomfortable driving situations, such as night driving, busy intersections and bad weather.

So it is possible that some senior drivers do tend to regulate themselves. As one researcher stated, "When drivers age they often drive more carefully." The study referenced above, however, showed that the effect of any compensating practices did not make the seniors better drivers. Instead, by practicing these strategies, they are really, in effect, lowering the level of difficulty or exposure to real driving situations.

The senior driver who recognizes a *"slow down"* should be moved to be more critical of their driving and really concentrate on the seriousness of the driving task so that other drivers are not adversely effected. It is this *"awareness"* that will make us smarter and safer drivers! Remember, keeping our drivers license and our privilege of driving is what we all want. What would we do without it?

The next chapter, "Crashes-Traffic Violations And The Senior Driver," will lead us into the need for each of us to become more aware of what some of our driving problems are and how we can correct them.

WHAT HAVE I LEARNED?

TRUE OR FALSE?

1. It is unsafe to drive too slowly?
2. Mirrors are a valuable tool and an aid to driving safely.
3. 50% of all traffic fatalities would have been injury-only crashes if those involved had been wearing seat belts.
4. Few crashes happen at intersections because they are so well controlled by signs that everyone obeys.
5. It is okay to use one foot on the accelerator and one foot on the brake because you can stop more quickly.
6. I have had more than one vehicle crash recently so I am not likely to have another one.
7. When tested on the meaning of signs, very few senior drivers failed to identify all of them.
8. A senior driver who is able to recognize that some of his reactions and reflexes are slowing down will be moved to concentrate more on the driving task.

ANSWERS:

1. True
2. True
3. True
4. False
5. False
6. False
7. False
8. True

Chapter Three

TRAFFIC VIOLATIONS – CRASHES AND THE SENIOR DRIVER

Some Key Points in this Chapter

- Is there an inter-relation between traffic violations and vehicle crashes?

- Factors most often cited in crashes involving senior drivers.

- Contributing factor in over 50% of senior crashes.

Chapter Three

TRAFFIC VIOLATIONS – CRASHES AND THE SENIOR DRIVER

WHO ME?

Unfortunately, many automobile crashes involving senior drivers have resulted from a senior driver actually violating a well-defined traffic regulation. There is a definite relationship between traffic violations and vehicle crashes. When a traffic investigator is writing out his or her incident report, or the Department of Public Safety Police Traffic Accident Report, the officer must indicate the *Pre-Accident Actions/Maneuvers* initiated by the involved motorists. He or she must also indicate the *Apparent Contributing Factor(s)*, illegal, improper, or unsafe actions that **in their professional opinion** were responsible for the crash.

These are the illegal, improper or unsafe actions or factors most often cited in crashes involving senior drivers. They are:

(1) **Failure To Yield Right-Of-Way**. The *Number 1 traffic violation* for senior drivers, 55 years of age and over. A contributing factor in 67.3% of all crashes involving drivers 65 years of age and older.
(2) **Inattention**.
(3) **Improper Turning**.
(4) **Improper Lane Change**.

In multiple vehicle crashes, two factors predominated over all the others: **Failure To Yield Right-Of-Way** and **Driver Inattention or Distraction**. In single vehicle crashes the factors most often cited were **Physical Impairment and/or Speed**.

By our drawing attention to just which violations and related crash contributing factors are most evident in the senior driving population, you will be able to recognize where you can contribute to a change in a growing public health problem, that of senior vehicle crashes.

What are the Safe Driving Tips that will help us cope with the Violation/Factors that effect our driving? The next chapter, "Safe Driving Tips For The Senior Driver" will be revealing.

WHAT HAVE I LEARNED?

TRUE OR FALSE?

1. There is absolutely no relationship between traffic violations and vehicle crashes.
2. The Number 1 traffic violation for senior drivers involved in crashes is failure to yield right-of- way.
3. Senior drivers are able to make a big contribution to a change in today's driving environment by recognizing which traffic violations and crash contributing factors are causing the most problems.

ANSWERS:

1. False
2. True
3. True

Chapter Four

SAFE DRIVING TIPS FOR THE SENIOR DRIVER

Some Key Points in this Chapter

- Factors associated with senior crashes.

- What is reaction time?

- A common misconception about reaction time.

- Why is reaction time so critical?

- Chart of reaction time and stopping distances.

- How many feet-per-second are you traveling?

- What happens when our field of vision narrows?

- Noticing vision changes.

- Use your headlights at all time. Why?

- Why didn't we hear that emergency vehicle siren?

- Why get a hearing evaluation?

- How many driving decisions do we make in just 5 miles?

- Are cell phones practical?

- Factors causing a delay in our deciding to act in an emergency.

Chapter Four

SAFE DRIVING TIPS FOR THE SENIOR DRIVER

REACTION TIME AND YOU

There are many senior drivers who are safer drivers than drivers half their age, but as we have seen, *aging certainly can have some negative effects on our ability to drive safely.*

The driving environment consists of many factors or cues to danger: roadway, other drivers, pedestrians, other vehicles, sun, nighttime, road shadows, inclement weather, snow/ice, etc. How do we react when one or more of these factors changes?

Reaction time, what is it? The **time lapse** between when we first see danger and our brain makes a decision and sends a message to our foot to apply the brake, is **reaction time**. Is our reaction time fast or slow? When we see another vehicle approaching our path from a side street, or swerving into our lane to avoid a child's ball that has rolled into the street, how do we react? How quickly and wisely will we make a decision when under this stress, and how quickly can we turn our decision into action in order to avoid a crash?

Generally, seniors have a slower reaction time. As our reaction time slows we can improve our chances of surviving, provided we unlearn a common myth some of us may have had for years. That common myth about crashes is, "When I see a crash coming I will be able to do **something** to protect myself and my passengers." The reality is that drivers seldom **"see"** a crash coming. Usually a crash is over before we realize that a crash has occurred.

Crashes are formed in 3 seconds or less with little time to react positively. That is why investigating officers often hear, "I don't know what happened," or "I didn't see them coming." With our human perception being what it is, limited, drivers usually do not at first know who hit whom. Not understanding the limited time one has, not understanding reaction time, **drivers allow far too little time margin for evasive action.**

If you are driving 30 mph, the ideal average reaction distance is 33 feet. Your vehicle has already traveled 33 feet closer to whatever danger you saw **before** your foot can leave the gas pedal and even come close to the brake pedal. Think of it, when you see the danger is it closer than 33 feet? If so, you will crash! If it is within 75 feet you have cut it very close, as the stopping distance of your vehicle at 30 mph is 73 feet.

Why is reaction distance so critical? Because our reaction time slows as we age! This is a fact we must face.

Safe Driving Tip: Be aware of the reaction time factor and how closely it is related to our ability to stop or take evasive action to avoid a crash!

CHART OF REACTION TIME AND STOPPING DISTANCES [1]

Driving Speed	Reaction Distance	Braking Distance	Total Stopping Distance	Elapsed Driving Time 10 miles
30 mph	33 feet	40 feet	73 feet	
40 mph	44 feet	72 feet	116 feet	
50 mph	60 feet	148 feet	209 feet	11 minutes
60 mph	66 feet	182 feet	248 feet	10 minutes
65 mph	71 feet	220 feet	291 feet	9 minutes
70 mph	77 feet	266 feet	343 feet	8 minutes

These are averages for light passenger vehicles on dry pavement. In other words, ideal conditions. *National Highway Traffic Safety Administration.*

Knowledge of time and distance when driving gets more serious when we begin to look at how many *feet per second* we have traveled at a certain speed. For example: When driving at 35 mph, we are traveling 51.3 feet per second. That is over *500 feet in 10 seconds*. At 55 mph, we are traveling 80.6 feet per second. That is over *800 ft in 10 seconds!*

We must realize, too, that "knowledge of time is of the essence when driving." Not, as some people think, that they must get where they are going as quickly as possible, by aggressive actions and without consideration for anyone else. Rather, in being aware of reaction time tables and knowing both reaction and stopping distances, we are able to cope with the various elements of our driving environment safely.

How many times haven't we been passed by a driver driving over 50 mph in a 35 mph zone and said, "There goes a driver on the way to a crash site, his own!"

---

[1] *Chart of reaction time and stopping distances* reflects the average of groups of cars. Braking distances may vary depending upon weight, design of vehicle, road condition, type of roadway and driver's condition.

Safe Driving Tip: **Driving** today is a "full time" job. Learn reaction times and distances. **Drive Defensively.** Remember that the other driver will probably NOT do what you expect them to do. **Be alert for the unexpected**. Keep a safe distance between you and the other drivers. (We'll talk more about that later.)

VISION CHANGES

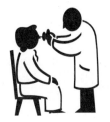

Most all of us have experienced some loss of visual sharpness as we age. Every driver, no matter what their age, knows that at dusk, on cloudy days, and during periods of rainy weather, many objects in the driving environment do not stand out well enough to be easily identified. As our field of vision narrows we are actually receiving and processing less and less visual information. The *National Institute of Aging* has published data indicating that drivers with less than 40% of normal vision were **6 times more likely** to become involved in vehicle crashes.

Seniors can help themselves become safer drivers by learning how vision changes affect driving and how to compensate for these changes. Following are some vision changes you may notice:
1. Needing more light to see well on overcast days.
2. Increased difficulty when changing focus from near to far.
3. Greater sensitivity to glare or bright sun light.
4. Diminished peripheral vision - the ability to see to our sides when looking straight ahead.
5. Difficulty distinguishing colors quickly and accurately.

It is surprising how many senior drivers do not realize their vision is not what it used to be, or have their eyes checked annually. While eye tests alone do not identify the riskiest drivers, recent media coverage has highlighted the important part poor vision has played in some very serious automobile crashes. With our useful field of vision diminishing, one research study found that drivers falling into this category were **15 times more likely** to become involved in intersection crashes.

Safe Driving Tips:
1. Visit your eye doctor regularly and keep your prescription up-to-date.
2. Wear quality sunglasses or prescription glasses, if needed.
3. Keep mirrors, headlights, tail lights, inside and outside of windshield, clean and in good repair.
4. Turn on your headlights when poor weather conditions are obvious. Some states require that headlights be on any time you use your windshield wipers.

Some countries manufacture cars that have **daytime running lights** (DRL's). Thankfully, some US manufacturers are now utilizing this feature on new vehicles.

Safe Driving Tip: *Use your headlights at all times whenever you drive. It is a safety tool that helps other drivers see you!*

Check your mirrors often, glancing from the road ahead to the rear view, side mirrors and then the road ahead, taking in the *"big picture."* Never wear sunglasses or tinted glasses for driving at night or at dusk.

Smart drivers use these Safe Driving Tips and steer clear of crashes!

HEARING

Many seniors experience some hearing loss as they age. They may be able to hear, but may not be able to clearly understand words. Just as our vision helps us monitor what is going on around us, so too, hearing well helps us sort out sounds important to the driving task.

When there is hearing loss we really cannot say we are "fully alert" to all the various elements in the driving environment. We may be able to get along, but are others avoiding or looking out for us? If we have a decreased sense of the intensity and volume of sound, how would we react if an emergency vehicle with its siren on approaches us from the rear or from a side street? Could we hear it and take proper action soon enough so we do not find ourselves in danger or end up a victim in another ambulance?

What can we do to respond positively if we notice that our hearing ability is reduced or has diminished measurably?

Safe Driving Tips:
1. Visit your physician and ask for a test. Some hearing aid companies even offer a free hearing evaluation to seniors. After an evaluation that indicates you are in need of a hearing aid, **get one!** It could save your life!
2. Background noise can be distracting. Keep your radio volume at a level so you can hear outside noise (i.e. emergency vehicles).
3. Using your mirrors will help to offset hearing loss.
4. Passenger conversation can be distracting and has been noted to be the cause of some driving problems, especially in traffic. Let your passengers be aware of this and, if necessary, ask them to limit their conversation.

Our hearing sense is a critical one if we are to survive in today's traffic.

DECIDING TO ACT

Maximizing our chances of staying on the road longer and safely by making the right driving decisions is no luxury. It is a necessity!

Drivers must make about **20 major decisions for every mile driven**, many of them in less than 20 seconds. If it is 5 miles to the mall you have probably made **100 major driving decisions**. Were they all correct ones?

If your mind wandered or if your attention was distracted by noise or by a passenger, you may not have made all the correct driving decisions somewhere along the way. Did another driver have to take some evasive action to avoid you? Each time our attention is distracted, it may be interfering with our driving safely.

What are some things that steal our attention? They are:
1. Being upset or stressed about a problem.
2. Anger about a family situation.
3. Not feeling up-to-par, drowsy or tired.
4. Too long behind the wheel on a trip, resulting in inattention.
5. Passenger conversation.
6. Radio talk shows.
7. Using a cell phone. [2]

---

[2]   Although we recommend that mature drivers purchase a cell phone for emergency use, please do not use it while operating your vehicle. If you must use the cell phone, **stop** your vehicle. Research has proven that drivers using cell phones have the **same risk of crashing as they would while driving with their blood alcohol level above the legal limit**.

When we are driving we pick up clues for action through our visual and auditory sensing abilities. Deciding to act is the result of correct processing of this information. After deciding to act, the driver must translate that decision into action, i.e. some combination of braking, steering, acceleration or some other kind of evasive action to avoid a crash.

A factor that can cause a delay in deciding to act is a senior driver's inability to process information rapidly and to respond correctly. Unfortunately, there are some among us who will not admit to the "slow down" attributable to age. "Who me? My driving ability is the same as it was 10 years ago." They are often a hazard to themselves and others.

While changes in driving habits can somewhat compensate for a senior's delayed response to a traffic problem, they do not always work. This is where it would be possible to become confused if the "cues" to an impending danger were rapid and/or limited - at a time when *speed* **and** *accuracy of response* are the only things that will save one from a crash.

If we have developed good driving habits, our response will probably be the correct one. Long-standing good habits continue to stay with us! Our need to make right decisions for survival is critical. Learn the driving strategies outlined in this guidebook !

WHAT HAVE I LEARNED?

TRUE OR FALSE?

1. Reaction time has to do with how quickly we start up when the light turns green.
2. Total stopping distance equals reaction distance plus braking distance.
3. A safety cushion is used for comfort on long trips.
4. Drivers with less than 40% of normal vision are 6 times more likely to be involved in car crashes.
5. Using our headlights at all times when we are driving helps other drivers see us.
6. Taking in the "big picture" includes using our mirrors.
7. Our hearing sense is not that critical to safe driving.
8. Drivers make 20 major driving decisions for every mile driven.
9. Never use the cell phone while operating your car.

ANSWERS:

1. False
2. True
3. False
4. True
5. True
6. True
7. False
8. True
9. True

Chapter Five

CORRECT DRIVING TECHNIQUES FOR SURVIVAL TO LIVE

Some Key Points in this Chapter

- Are crashes beyond a driver's control?

- What does driving defensively mean?

- What is the prerequisite to changing old driving habits?

- Right-Of-Way - When to yield it.

- Overtaking or meeting a school bus. What now?

- Right-Of-Way rules.

- Red light rules-right turn on red.

- Left turning - How to correctly and legally.

- Passing - No passing.

- Lane Changes - How to . . .

- Parking legally.

- Backing – When not to back up.

- Entering a freeway.

- Do seat belts really save lives? Who do *not* have to wear them?

- Examples of inattentive driving.

Chapter Five

CORRECT DRIVING TECHNIQUES FOR SURVIVAL TO LIVE

Myth: Motor vehicle collisions or crashes are the result of something beyond the driver's control.

Talk to a driver who has just been involved in a collision, and for the most part they will attribute the crash to: weather, lights or sun in my eyes, bad road, silly teenage driver, some old driver, "phantom" car, etc. Let's not make the other driver the bad guy, maybe we did make mistake. There is usually a mental error or misjudgment on one or both drivers' part. One of them was caught not trying to avoid a collision.

Safe driving means driving defensively. Driving defensively means ***not*** expecting other drivers to do the right thing. Thinking to yourself, "that guy approaching the stop sign may not stop, is going to turn left in front of me, is going to cut me off, may hit his brakes at any time." Driving defensively also means making all our turns from the correct lane, automatically signaling all our turns, and knowing what right-of-way means and when to use it. In other words, driving defensively means concentrating on our driving all the time." Drive with your guard up - drive smart!

How many of us are willing to admit that perhaps we are not driving as safely as we could be? Our driving can be improved with lasting benefits to others, as well as to ourselves. ***We are as safe behind the wheel as we are determined to be!***

Our goal in this guidebook is to provide a review of basic Safe Driving Tips along with some awareness teaching. These will help develop a sub-conscious awareness that will raise your driving safety probability above that of the less informed driver, and help you retain your license and independence.

Correct and clear knowledge is a prerequisite to changing old habits!

RIGHT-OF-WAY

Technically, the law does not give anyone the right-of-way. It only says who must yield it. Right-of-way rules help traffic flow smoothly and safely, but also are an aid in fixing blame in vehicle crashes. The defensive driving emphasis is on common sense and courtesy. It's simply smart driving.

One thing stands out foremost . . . *"never insist on taking the right-of-way."* Even if you are right, never put that thinking ahead of your safety. It is a small victory if you are able to tell those visiting you in the hospital, "but I had the right-of-way!"

When another driver does not follow the rules, we cannot act as traffic judge. Let him have the right-of-way even if, technically, it belongs to you.

WHEN TO YIELD RIGHT-OF-WAY

1. When a light turns green and pedestrians and vehicles are still in the intersection.

2. When a blind person is crossing in front of you.

3. When you start from a parked position at the curb and intend to enter moving traffic.

4. Whenever you meet or overtake a school bus that is stopped and has *FLASHING RED LIGHTS AND AN EXTENDED 'STOP' ARM*. Remain stopped until red lights are turned off and the 'stop' arm is down.

5. When entering any highway or street from an alley, driveway or farm yard.

6. Yield to all emergency vehicles:
   - Approaching from front, rear or from the side street, and are displaying red lights and sounding a siren.
   - On a two-lane road with traffic moving in both directions, pull over to the right and stop.
   - On a one way roadway pull over to the side of the road or curb nearest to your vehicle and stop.
   - If in an intersection you should quickly clear it before stopping.
   - Remain stopped until all emergency vehicles have passed.

SOME RIGHT-OF-WAY RULES

1. When two vehicles on different roadways approach an intersection not controlled by signs or signals, the driver on the *left* should yield to the driver on the right.
2. When the intersection is controlled by signs or by blinking signals, the driver of the vehicle on the *left* should yield to the driver on the right.
3. When there are stop signs at all four corners of an intersection, every driver must make *a complete stop.* The driver who stopped first goes first. Eye contact is important. Never assume you have the right-of-way. Expect you will not be given the right-of-way, even when it is yours.

RED LIGHT RULES

1. Complete stops are required behind the crosswalk and before entering the intersection (See additional tips in 10 Most Infamous Driving Behaviors - Failure To Yield Right-Of-Way).
2. RIGHT ON RED. A **complete stop** is required and right-of-way **must** be given to any crossing traffic. Other approaching vehicles have the green light and the right-of-way. The approaching vehicle should not have to slow down and yield to a vehicle turning right on red. You should remain stopped until all vehicles have passed through the intersection.

Has this law compromised safety? The law was supposed to help traffic flow and it does, but it is up to us to reduce the risks. We read the law as stop, turn right on red when you have the right of way. **Because you can does not mean you should!**

ON THE GREEN

When entering an intersection "on the green" and you intend turning to the left, you should **proceed into the intersection** to the point where your left turn would be made, and stop. You must yield to pedestrians or vehicles already legally within the intersection, or so close to prove a hazard to the safe completion of your left turn. Complete your turn when safe to do so.

Right-of-way rules permit a driver to complete a left turn on red, provided he or she is already in the intersection.

We see many drivers turning left on the green who do not move forward into the intersection in preparation for their turn. Some wait at or even behind the crosswalk for the signal to change and then make their turn on the yellow light. This leaves no time for any other driver behind them to complete their left turn without doing so on the red light. This can have disastrous results.

Consideration for other drivers would require that we move forward into the intersection to the position from which our left turn would be made, then complete the turn when safe to do so.

Safe Driving Tip: If another driver insists on the right-of-way, give in. Always yield the right-of-way, even if you are entitled to it. Contending with another driver over who has the right-of-way can be a losing battle.

TURNING

There are definite laws that regulate how a driver must make a turn, and failure to make a proper turn can actually result in a traffic citation, or worse a collision.

Making wide right turns or cutting the corner on left turns are just simply bad habits and they should be avoided and corrected. Any time we are turning or changing position on a roadway we must **communicate our intentions to other drivers** well in advance of when we intend to make our turn, **by signaling**.

LEFT TURNS

Smart, safety conscious older drivers know that the combination of intersections and left turns can spell trouble.

If you are not comfortable with making left turns in certain locations than **avoid them**. Familiarize yourself with routes that will provide signalized left turn arrows. Then too, one can take an extra minute by driving one extra block and make a series of three right turns. This will put you on the same street and same course that your one "uncomfortable" left turn would have put you on.

Never turn your wheels to the left while waiting in an intersection for oncoming traffic to clear before making your turn. More than one driver has been rear-ended while waiting and pushed left into the oncoming traffic. Finish your turn by entering the street in the first lane right of the center line. Then signal and move over to the right lane.

Safe Driving Tip: Always get as close to the center line as possible on your approach to a left turn . . . the same distance as your signal, one hundred feet.

PASSING

A key question to ask yourself before passing another vehicle: "Is this pass actually necessary"? What are you going to do with the very few extra seconds gained by making an unsafe pass? Why not wait until you are sure it is safe to pass? Too many serious and fatal crashes are the result of improper passing.

Improper passing is a violation of common sense, and of the law. Keep a ***three-second following distance*** between you and any car you intend to pass. This will enable you to see far enough ahead and ensure safely passing them.

Be alert for the solid yellow center stripe in your lane and for NO PASSING signs.

DO NOT PASS WHEN:
1. Solid yellow line is in your lane.
2. You cannot see ahead of you clearly for a distance of 700 feet.
3. When approaching a curve or hill.
4. Within 100 feet of any traffic intersection.
5. Crossing a railroad track or approaching a tunnel or bridge.

PASSING ON THE RIGHT

There are only *three* situations when passing on the right is permitted:
1. When the vehicle in front of you is making a left turn. Do not leave the pavement to do this. Some roadways, however, are being widened and marked to permit passing on the right.
2. On a one-way street.
3. On any roadway that has clearly marked multiple lanes of traffic going in the same direction.

Remember, anytime you are passing or overtaking another vehicle and you cannot see the face of the driver in his/her rear view mirror, you are in his/her blind spot.

Safe Driving Tip: Every vehicle has ***blind spots***. Check yours by ***turning your head*** and looking over your shoulder.

PASSING A TRUCK

When passing a truck, wait until you can see the front of the truck in your rear-view mirror, signal, and move back into the right lane. Passing semi-trucks is not usually a concern, as they are usually traveling at speeds far in excess of posted limits.

When sharing the roadway with trucks, drive defensively! Never drive alongside a truck for any distance, or sandwiched between two trucks.

Few survive a collision with an 18 wheel, 48,000-pound "weapon," driven in excess of the speed limit. It is not our intention to paint all truckers with the same brush, but as in any industry there are a few truckers who make it difficult for others with exemplary safety records.

The moral of the story is: ***Give trucks plenty of room!***

LANE CHANGES

Recall that in the chapter covering those factors accounting for some of the highest numbers of vehicle crashes we learned that a simple lane change, when done in an improper way, was the cause of a high percentage of collisions.

Changing lanes can be dangerous and must be done with caution. Many lane changing crashes are due to *lack of communication*. Changing lanes without using a signal or from the wrong lane is inexcusable, and requires other drivers to make a split-second decision to avoid us. Sometimes their reaction time is not fast enough, and a crash happens.

What is good communication when changing a lane or position on the roadway? Good communication has two elements:
1. Begin to position your vehicle far in advance of your lane change by getting into the correct lane. This is called ***"position signaling"***.
2. Signal your intention to make a lane change ***before*** you start to make the change, ***not*** after you have started the lane change. This is good communication!

Safe Driving Tip: Begin to make a lane change only **after** you have checked for safe clearance to the side, behind, and ahead of your vehicle. This will ensure you can make the change safely.

Remember, a turn signal *does not give you the "right"* to make a lane change. Every day we see drivers cut in front of another driver and signal afterwards. This is irresponsible and inexcusable. **You must be alert and considerate and wait until it is safe to make a lane change!** A skilled driver will not change his or her lane position when unsure of traffic.

Also, be alert to make sure your turn signal is turned off. Perhaps the lane change did not involve enough steering wheel turn to cancel the signal automatically. If not, then visually check to see that your signal is off.

PARKING

Comfortable with parallel parking? If not, avoid high risk parking in heavy traffic areas. Pay for valet parking or use a lot and walk two blocks. If you are like me, you need it, even when it hurts!

High-risk parking includes:
1. Any parking at corners of an intersection.
2. In alleyways or driveways.
3. The end spaces in shopping malls where vehicles are turning.
4. Any place a turning vehicle may crash into your car.
5. Parking right next to a van. (Statistics show that people often use vans to commit crimes in parking lots).
6. Parking on a hill without turning your wheels.
   - Wheels should be turned toward the curb or shoulder when facing down a hill.
   - Wheels should be turned away from curb when facing up a hill.
   - Wheels should be turned toward shoulder when no curb is available.
7. Parking on the wrong side of the street.

Illegal parking includes:
1. Any crosswalk, driveway or bridge.
2. Double-parking alongside a legally parked vehicle.
3. At a yellow or red marked curb.
4. At bus stops.
5. 10 feet from a fire hydrant.
6. 20 feet from an alley or intersection.
7. 30 feet from a stop sign-or any traffic control device.
8. On a freeway.
9. At curbside when the wheels are beyond 12 inches from the curb.
10. On the wrong side of the street, facing traffic.

Note: Consult your own State Driver's Manual for these parking rules in your area.

BACKING

Unsafe backing contributes to a significant number of reported and unreported crashes. This is unnecessary! **ALL backing crashes are preventable!**

Using your mirror while backing is dangerous. This is where exercise comes in. If you are having difficulty turning your head you must exercise those muscles. Practice looking over your shoulder, turning your body, and looking back behind you.

Important rule: Look behind you the entire time you are backing, and back slowly.

Over the years I have seen many drivers who use the **"back by sound"** method. It's simple. Put the transmission into reverse and back up until you hear the crashing sound of hitting the car behind you. This is not an acceptable driving practice, and your friendly Driver License Examiner will mark your score sheet, "Fail."

Never back up:
1. When you are on a controlled access or interstate highway.
2. If you miss an exit. (Drive on to the next one, it could mean your life!)
3. Across traffic lanes.
4. Into an intersection.
5. Around a corner.
6. More than five car lengths in a roadway.

Remember, some of these actions could result in a traffic citation.

If you must back out of a driveway, always back into the nearest lane, not across two lanes, and then proceed forward from there. After making sure there are no pedestrians or objects behind your vehicle, and having carefully checked your mirrors, look back over your shoulder the entire time you are backing.

Safe Driving Tip: Back into a parking space when you first arrive. This will enable you to see that no one is behind you. Then when you are ready to leave you can pull forward to exit the parking space. This is not only easier, but much safer!

Whenever you change the position of your transmission selector from Park to Reverse, or from Park to Drive, or Drive to Reverse, *put your foot on the brake and hold it until you have made the change and are ready to proceed*. After making the change, have you checked clearance around your vehicle? Is it safe to proceed? Has anyone walked behind your car since the last time you checked?

Some seniors have the reputation of being careless about backing. Be careful that you do not join that group. *Remember that backing crashes do not have to happen!*

DRIVING ON INTERSTATE FREEWAYS

Most of the suggestions for driving safely on interstate roadways apply also to parkways, expressways, thruways and turnpikes, depending on where we reside. We are going to use the term freeway to be consistent.

It is likely that many senior drivers often wish they did not have to drive the freeways, and this may be a legitimate concern for some. With driving at the close of the 20th Century becoming more dangerous, if you can get to your destination without exposing yourself to the aggressive and sometimes irresponsible drivers who seem to be taking over our roadways, then you might do well to consider that. However, at the same time you must consider that you lose the benefits derived from these safer roadways.

Our research shows freeways have a much lower fatality rate than conventional highways. Because of this it would seem that it may be beneficial to use them. But when we do, we must bring ourselves "up to speed" in knowledge and awareness of proper and acceptable methods.

One aspect that seems to be the most difficult for some seniors is getting on and off the freeway. What are some things we can do to make using the freeway easier?

ENTERING A FREEWAY

Planning and communication are vital, especially when entering a freeway. Freeways have an acceleration lane and you must increase your speed to match that of other vehicles on the roadway. Your signal should be activated as you begin your acceleration. Watch the vehicle in front of you. Rear end crashes occur on ramps because drivers fail to notice a driver ahead of them has hesitated or stopped.

While merging it is vital that you keep an eye on freeway traffic and check for gaps in traffic that will allow you to enter. This is the tricky part. Remember that we must yield to traffic already on the freeway. If slowing down due to heavy freeway traffic is necessary, start slowing early, perhaps halfway on the ramp, so you will still have space ahead to find your gap and enter at freeway speed.

Entering a freeway requires precision and practice, so it is not out of the realm of reason to actually practice entering the freeway . . . but please don't pick morning or evening rush hour traffic!

LEAVING A FREEWAY

More advance planning and communication is needed:
1. Move to the proper exit lane far in advance of leaving the freeway.
2. Signal your intention to leave the freeway.
3. Maintain freeway speed. **NEVER slow or brake before reaching the exit ramp.**
4. When you reach the exit ramp, start slowing and let your car slow without sudden braking.
5. Observe the speed limit on exit ramp. (Traffic engineers have determined the safe exit ramp speed.)

Note: If you miss your exit, **never stop and back up**. Go on to the next exit and save a life! Also, do not use the median crossover lanes (U-turn slots) reserved for maintenance and emergency vehicles.

Safe Driving Tip: When you can see another vehicle about to merge from a ramp acceleration lane and there is no gap for it to merge into traffic, *create one by momentarily reducing your speed.* This is called "courtesy," old-fashioned and out of style, but refreshing.

WHY SEAT BELTS? BUCKLE UP!

Many of us started to drive when there were no seat belts in cars, so the thought of belting ourselves into our cars was not received with enthusiasm. Some have said they "just never got in the habit." In fact, this is one habit some adamantly refuse to develop. They say, "what would happen if we drove into a lake or our vehicle caught on fire, we would never survive." The attitude of many 'old timers' is "damn the belts." Those of you with that frame of mind are fooling yourselves that you are safer without a three-point belt restraint. Statistics prove you wrong. The likelihood of you losing your life **as a result of wearing your seat belt** is extremely low. So buckle up!

Over the past 40 years I have monitored vehicle fatalities in Minnesota. In many, many cases it was noted that the people killed were NOT wearing seat belts. Many of them were thrown from their vehicles upon impact, causing fatal head injuries. Countless studies and literally thousands of graphic accounts have proven that using seat belts reduces the risk of death and serious injury by 40% to 60%. Immortality does not extend to senior drivers or the occupants of their cars who do not or will not buckle up.

Scientific evidence proves that there are other beneficial effects to drivers and occupants who wear their seat belts. People wearing seat belts reduce the chance of **secondary collision** injuries. Secondary collision injuries are those caused by your body or head striking the inside of your car, windshield, etc., or being thrown from the vehicle. Oftentimes these secondary collisions are more deadly than the initial collision.

A study undertaken by the state of New York, *"The Highway & Vehicle Safety Report,"* found that **unbelted drivers** **double** their risk of suffering any type of injury, and **triple** the risk of experiencing head injury. They also are **twice** as likely to need emergency room treatment. Furthermore, average hospital charges for individuals involved in a motor vehicle crash is $11,200 for unbelted drivers, compared to $7,600 for belted drivers.

WHO DO NOT HAVE TO WEAR A SEAT BELT
Any person while:
1. Driving a vehicle in reverse.
2. Exempted by medical certificate.
3. Delivering U.S. Mail.
4. Engaged in normal farm work.
5. Driving a vehicle manufactured prior to 1965.
6. Involved in work that requires exiting and entering a vehicle frequently.

All states and provinces require that vehicles be equipped with seat belts and that all drivers and passengers wear "properly adjusted and fastened seat belts." This is a law, not just on the highway or on a trip, but also when going to the store!

Grandparents! Are you putting your young grandchildren at risk by NOT requiring them to be safely and properly belted when they are your responsibility? Do not let "Johnny" tell you he does not like to wear a seat belt. It is **your** responsibility when they are in your care.

Both the *Insurance Institute for Traffic Safety* and *The National Highway Traffic Safety Administration (NHTSA)* recommend that children be seated in the back seat and belted. Why? Because children, 12 years of age and younger, who are seated in the rear of the vehicle, have a 35% lower risk of fatal injury than those seated in the front seat.

We now know that research done by the NHTSA and by many other organizations proves that seniors are more likely to be injured or killed in motor vehicle crashes than younger persons are. Therefore, we cannot overemphasize the importance of all drivers and passengers properly using the three-point shoulder and lap belt at all times.

BUCKLE UP AND LIVE LONGER!

INATTENTION

You have been doing this "driving thing" for a long time, but let's hope you have not let it become a "part-time" job. If there is one basic rule, it is this: *Confine any inattention or side activity, like sightseeing, to uncomplicated traffic situations and when driving at a very low speed.*

Some remarkable stories have been conjured up as reasons for single vehicle **"solo crashes,"** such as driving over a curb, hitting a parked car, backing into a building or another car, hitting a post or railing when turning or backing, etc. We must acknowledge that practically all **"solo crashes"** represent some kind of inattention and lack of vehicle control.

Examples of inattentive driving include:

1. Train/Motor Vehicle crashes. Being inattentive to the possibilities of a collision with a train is a sad way to end a nice quiet ride in the country or a trip to your favorite resort!

2. Not paying attention to speedometer readings. Yes, some of us seniors think very little about stopping distances. That old habit of "driving with traffic", even under treacherous road conditions, carries over from dry-surface driving to slippery-surface driving. Some of us pay no attention to conditions and drive 30 mph on icy snow-packed streets. There is no tread on any tire or any four-wheel drive vehicle that will guarantee safety on a slippery surface. Remember, too, there is no stop sign or red light that has ever stopped a sliding, out-of-control vehicle!

WHAT HAVE I LEARNED?

TRUE OR FALSE?

1. Driving defensively means NOT expecting the other driver to do the right thing every time.
2. When the right-of-way belongs to us we should react positively and take it.
3. A school bus with flashing yellow lights is expecting you to stop.
4. Communicating our intentions to other drivers means we signal for all changes in our traffic position.
5. Defensive driving includes keeping plenty of space between ourselves and trucks.
6. We can make a lane change anytime we signal for it.
7. All backing crashes are preventable.
8. Freeways give us the benefit of being safer roadways to drive on.
9. It is okay to slow down on a freeway if we are going to exit soon.
10. Seat belts reduce the risk of injury and death by 40-60%.
11. A complete stop is required before we can turn right on red.
12. A 'second collision' is when our vehicle strikes another vehicle after the first collision.
13. "Solo" crashes are those where there are no other passengers in your car.

ANSWERS:

1. True
2. False
3. False
4. True
5. True
6. False
7. True
8. True
9. False
10. True
11. True
12. False
13. False

Chapter Six

CRASH PREVENTION TIPS AND DRIVING DECISIONS

Some Key Points in this Chapter

- Failure to yield right-of-way is the cause of 1/3 of all intersection crashes.

- What to do when starting through an intersection.

- Taking a defensive position at the green light.

- Yellow light - the most misunderstood signal.

- Running a red light.

- Right turn on red. When?

- A distraction in your vehicle?

- Full-time attention to our driving.

- Do we visualize lanes when they are not marked? Why?

- Traffic control signs have never stopped every driver.

- Are we backing up without looking?

- What is position signaling?

- Is there an orange triangle on the back of your vehicle?

- The safe level of alcohol in our system.

Chapter Six

CRASH PREVENTION TIPS AND DRIVING DECISIONS

A motor vehicle collision without a "preventable" mistake is rare!

We senior drivers will make progress in our ability to be safer drivers if we are able to recognize the driving mistakes we may be making and become aware of what we can do to correct them. Also, we would do well to use the crash prevention tips outlined throughout this guide.

Our hope is that by listing the ***10 most infamous driving behaviors***, and the driving steps you must make to correct them, you will be aided in assessing your own driving skill. All of this will assist you in accomplishing the ***goal of driving longer and more safely!***

If we will do some honest self-scrutiny of our driving we may conclude that not understanding the factors causing vehicle crashes may sometimes be putting us in a precarious driving position. In any event, are other drivers having to watch out for us or avoid us? Let's hope not!

You are on the brink of a lawsuit every time you drive your car. Just think about that for a moment!

We are going to talk about some of our old bad habits and cover some very sensitive areas. Our goal is to increase your self-awareness so that you will become a ***safer senior driver***. Also, you will be more likely to retain your driving privilege when the time comes for taking a driver's license test . . . and it will come! There are many driving errors or behaviors that are causing most vehicle crashes. Some of these are the result of long-standing bad habits, but that also means they can be corrected.

Let's look at the 10 most infamous driving behaviors!

10 MOST INFAMOUS DRIVING BEHAVIORS

These behaviors are based on contributing factors, by percent, of single and multiple vehicle crashes within the 65-75 and older age group. *Minnesota Motor Vehicle Crash Facts, Department of Public Safety.*

No. 1.   Failure to yield right-of-way.

No. 2.   Inattention and/or distraction.

No. 3.   Turning from improper lane.

No. 4.   Ignoring or coasting through stop signs.

No. 5.   Backing.

No. 6.   Failure to position vehicle correctly for turning.

No. 7.   Changing lanes with no signal.

No. 8.   Lane straddling.

No. 9.   Driving too slowly.

No.10.   Driving after drinking.

INFAMOUS DRIVING BEHAVIOR NO. 1

FAILURE TO YIELD RIGHT-OF-WAY

Our failure to yield the right-of-way, and properly handle traffic situations at intersections, is the cause of nearly 1/3 of all crashes. When you think about it, intersections are really very dangerous places. Why?

Consider this:
1. Traffic can move in several directions at the same time. Some turning, some stopping, some starting, and some slowing.
2. An unforeseen occurrence can appear without warning.
3. Some vehicles are unable to stop due to speed or weather conditions.
4. Many aggressive, inconsiderate drivers refuse to stop, slow down or even look for other traffic.
5. Emergencies can develop suddenly.

Nevertheless, there are many drivers who are seemingly oblivious to the dangers of intersections and never adjust their speed or thinking to take into account the possibility of problems. I think they suffer from the "it can't happen to me" syndrome. To avoid problems driving through intersections we must drive defensively, fully expecting any of the conditions above to occur at any time.

There are two basic and constant rules to follow if we are to avoid a collision in an intersection:

Rule No. 1: The "No Right-of-Way Rule."
Never assume the other driver will yield, even when you have the right-of way.

Rule No. 2: The "Left, Right, Left Rule."
Before proceeding through an intersection, whether you have the right-of-way or not, **look first to the left, then to the right, then to the left again, before proceeding**. Turn your head to look. Do not just take a quick glance, you may miss an oncoming vehicle.

INTERSECTIONS WITH TRAFFIC CONTROL SIGNALS

Green light:

As you approach an intersection where the light has been green for awhile and is now "stale," get ready for the light to change to yellow.

"Cover" the brake.   Be prepared to stop!   What do we mean, "cover" the brake? Take your foot off the accelerator and place it over the brake pedal. Do not press on the brake pedal; just have your foot ready.   You have just shortened your reaction time by at least ¾ of a second, and your total stopping distance by 33 feet, if you are driving 30 mph. (Refer to the Chart of Reaction Time and Stopping Distances on page 24).

Allow an extra space between your car and the car in front of you. Take a *defensive position*.   Why? Will congestion ahead force the car in front of you to brake suddenly?   Will the signal change to yellow cause the car ahead to brake suddenly? (Not everyone drives through yellow lights).

When the red light turns to green, and *before* you start forward, *look both ways to see that cross traffic has stopped*. A vehicle from either side may speed through after their green light has changed to red. If you do not look both ways before starting through an intersection, you are inviting a car crash!

Yellow Light

A yellow light indicates a signal change, and allows you time to clear an intersection *when you are already driving through it, not when you are approaching it*. The yellow light signal is the most misunderstood signal and is generally abused by most drivers. The law is quite clear regarding driving through a yellow light:

" . . . vehicular traffic shall *not* enter the intersection".
MS 169.06 Subd. 5(b)(1) (Emphasis added).

Most every driver's manual states: **"Do not enter the intersection if you can stop safely before doing so. If you cannot stop safely, *move through with caution."*** (Emphasis added).

It is not unusual to see drivers who would have plenty of time to stop safely actually accelerate and speed through the intersection *after the signal has turned red.* We call these drivers *"chiselers."*

Your awareness and anticipation of the "stale" green light will enable you to make a smooth stop on the yellow and eliminates the need for hard braking.

Red Light

State law requires a ***complete stop*** at the stop line behind the crosswalk, or before entering the intersection. Running a red light is a characteristic of the overly aggressive and belligerent driving attitudes of many drivers today. This has an effect on our driving environment and exposes all of us to yet another danger.

In one recent study covered on national TV it was noted that, ***"drivers who run red lights kill 850 people a year and cause 260,000 crashes."*** In just one state, 36,000 citations were issued to those aggressive drivers who failed to stop for red lights. Nationally, it has been conservatively estimated that drivers running red lights have contributed to more than **250,000 intersection crashes**. And, believe it or not, there are some drivers out there who say we do not have a problem.

Recently some cities have installed cameras at intersections to record the plate numbers of drivers who run red lights. An outcry has come up from these *"chiselers"* who say this is an invasion of their rights. *Tell that to the family of someone killed by an aggressive driver who ran a red light!*

Right Turn on Red

Drivers do not have the "right" to turn right on every red light. Right turns on red are only allowed under certain conditions and then only with extreme caution. Remember that this has to do with right-of-way.

Turning right on red is allowed when:
1. No sign prohibits a right on red.
1. Your vehicle has **come to a complete stop** in the right hand lane. The Minnesota Statute clearly states that you: " . . . may make a right turn *after stopping...*" MS.169.06. (Emphasis added).
2. There is no oncoming traffic approaching the intersection that would have the right-of-way. Oncoming traffic should not have to slow down while you are making your right turn.
3. There are no pedestrians in the crosswalk or who are about to start crossing the intersection.

Note: Check the laws in your state regarding right turns on red.

Intersections controlled by STOP signs

A driver who has stopped at a stop sign must yield the right-of-way. There will be no intersection collision if the driver who has stopped does not force another driver on a through street to stop.

Right-Of Way and Yielding

Violation of right-of way rules is a major cause of traffic crashes. It is smart driving to obey these rules. They are just plain common sense and a part of **driving defensively**.

Let's review the rules again:

1. When two vehicles on different roadways approach an intersection **not controlled** by signs or signals at about the same time the rule is, "the driver of the vehicle on the left shall yield right-of-way to the driver on the right."
   Note: Any driver loses the right-of-way when he approaches an intersection at an unlawful speed.

2. When two vehicles on different roadways approach an intersection that is **controlled** by stop signs or by a blinking red light, the driver of the vehicle on the left shall yield right-of-way to the driver on the right.

3. When a vehicle approaches an intersection where there is a yield sign facing the driver, the **driver must slow down and stop,** if necessary, to yield to approaching or cross traffic.

4. When a vehicle enters an intersection on a **"left turn on green"** signal, the driver must yield to other vehicles already legally within the intersection or so close that it would pose a danger if he/she proceeded without yielding right-of way. When safe to do so, he/she may move to complete the left turn.

5. Whenever a transit bus is attempting to leave the curb and proceed to enter the right hand lane, as indicated by a flashing turn signal, a driver approaching in the right lane must yield the right-of way to the bus.

INATTENTION/DISTRACTION

Inattention plays a big part in the crash picture. There is so much going on around us. More traffic, more children playing in the streets, more pedestrians, more bicyclists, and more young and aggressive drivers who have that "get out of my way" attitude. Yes, the driving environment has changed appreciably, which should cause us to concentrate more fully on the driving task.

If there is one basic rule for those of us senior drivers it is to confine any distractions or side activities to those times when we are driving at a low speed.

Some bad habits evident among many senior drivers are:
1. Concentrating too long on oncoming vehicles so that they miss another vehicle or some other important factor affecting their driving.
2. Spending too much time looking in the rear view mirror, looking at a passenger when they are talking, or looking too long at what is going on around them. Our attention should be concentrated on the road ahead, not on the things going on around us.

It is extremely important to take in the *"big picture"* of what is going on around us, not just watching the rear bumper of the vehicle ahead of us. This allows us to be aware of events and traffic *far enough ahead* so that we can make proper adjustments or take corrective action. Paying *"more than the usual attention"* is vital, especially when driving at highway speeds. Only a few seconds of inattention can place us in a potentially dangerous situation. Gazing off in the distance or looking at sights of interest off the roadway when driving at highway speed must be eliminated.

If a distraction occurs within your vehicle, such as dropping a map or other object, stop your vehicle before dealing with it! Pay attention or pay! Be aware that **"Inattentive Driving"** has been added to the basic speed rule in the State of Minnesota. This law is intended to make all drivers more responsible for paying attention and adjusting their speed to the driving environment such as rain, fog, etc. If a driver was reading a map, a book, shaving, eating or drinking something prior to a crash, and his attention was not on the roadway, an investigating officer may issue that driver a citation.

You may say, "Don't kid me, how could anyone possibly shave while driving"? The California Highway Patrol recently released information from a study on inattentive driving. The study found that after collisions tickets were issued to drivers for things such as: reading a book, shaving while using a shaving mug and brush, playing a guitar, applying make up, combing hair, reading a newspaper, changing nylon stockings, using a cell phone, etc. In view of this information, we have to add these kinds of drivers to our list of persons we may be exposed to while attempting to get to our destination safely.

We can no longer take it for granted that our years of experience are going to see us through, compensating for the changed driving environment. Part of our preparation for driving safely today is to have a sub-conscious awareness of which situations are most likely to expose us to a collision.

What does this add up to? ***Giving our full time attention to the driving task***, and having knowledge and a respect for any possible situation that could pose a problem to our arriving at our destination safely.

When the day of our driving test arrives, Driver Examiners are going to look at how we pay attention. Points will be deducted on our examination if they detect any inattention on our part. For example: Do we look right and left when driving through an intersection? Do we look over our left shoulder when driving away from the curb? Do we turn our head and look to the rear while backing? These are all things they look for.

INFAMOUS DRIVING BEHAVIOR NO. 3

TURNING FROM IMPROPER LANE

Unfortunately, this infamous behavior stems from just plain "sloppy" driving and is the cause of a high ratio of unnecessary collisions. Simply put, if one or both drivers are turning from or into the proper lane, the possibility of a collision would be minimized or even eliminated.

Where are we on the street or roadway? Do we visualize lanes on the roadway even if none are marked?

Right Turn

 After signaling **at least 100 feet before a turn** we should move into the right hand lane closest to the curb. Make the turn and enter the street next to the curb or right hand lane. Never swing wide or drift to the left as you approach or before you turn right.

Left Turn

After checking traffic on your left side, signal and make a definite move into the lane next to the centerline. (All lanes of traffic are interfered with while making this turn). Your turn must be completed in the corresponding lane of the street from which the turn is made, i.e. the lane next to the centerline. This proper left turn allows another vehicle to occupy the right lane at the same time you are turning. A left turn from a right lane may mean crashing into another vehicle while turning.

After completion of your turn, and when safe to do so, it is appropriate to signal your intention, check your mirrors and traffic, and then change back into the right hand lane. A safe driver will neither "cut" a corner or make any turn from a wrong lane.

Important Rule: Left turners must **always** yield the right-of-way!

IGNORING OR COASTING THROUGH STOP SIGNS

Sad to say, too many experienced drivers are engaging in this inexcusable behavior. Could it be that the poor example older drivers have set contributed to the recent headline; "Young (40 year old) driver ignores stop sign, broadsiding vehicle carrying four, killing two."

How can we expect future drivers to stop for signs or signals when they watch parents ignore or coast through stop signs? From my perspective the word stop, or the red signal, does not mean "slow & go." Any driver who fails to come to a **complete stop** at a sign or signal when no police are present, are a part of the **"chiseler"** group I spoke about earlier. Scoffing at this law will eventually cause them to be involved in, or expose them as the cause of, a crash.

How can two vehicles crash at an intersection where there are traffic controls installed? I have never been able to come up with an answer to that question. Both drivers could not have proceeded correctly and safely at the same time and had a collision. *Somebody had to engage in Notorious Behavior No. 4.*

Safe Driving Tip: A red light or a stop sign has never stopped every driver. Take traffic controls seriously. The driver who has stopped must yield right-of-way. The first rule of right-of-way is that *every driver must make a reasonable effort to avoid a collision.*

When you have the green light, are you positive the driver on the opposing street with the red signal will stop? Have they seen it? Are they one of the drivers who scoff at the law and have no intention of stopping?

Drive defensively! When the light turns green *look both ways before you start forward.*

What about the amber or yellow light? How do drivers interpret them? Is it a signal to stop? Is it a signal to accelerate? You would never find the correct answer to that one by watching others at a traffic-controlled intersection! The Basic Rule requires that we *do not enter* an intersection on the yellow light *if we can stop safely before doing so*. (This is discussed in more detail under the heading; Yellow Light, Page 52).

<u>Safe Driving Tip</u>: When you are stopped at a stop signal, remember that when the light changes to green *you must look both ways before starting ahead*.

Not checking for cross traffic will expose you to that *"chiseler"* who is driving through the intersection on the red. It happens every day !

Drive defensively. Don't become a statistic!

INFAMOUS DRIVING BEHAVIOR NO. 5

BACKING

ALL backing collisions are preventable!

This bad behavior ranks high on the list of senior driver crash problems. There are some things each of us want to do when backing:

1. Are you sure you have looked to make sure there is nothing behind your vehicle . . . a child, a pedestrian, a bicycle?
2. Are you turning your torso around and looking to the rear before and during the time you are backing?
3. Are you backing slowly?
4. Are you sure your foot is on the brake? Most vehicles will move in reverse *without* use of the accelerator. Keeping your foot on the brake while backing will allow you more control of your vehicle.

Safe Driving Tip: Do not put your transmission selector in the reverse position and back up while looking in the rear view mirror!

Backing without looking is very dangerous, somewhat like playing Russian roulette. Some Driver License Examiners call it **"backing by sound,"** i.e. drivers backing up until they hear something they have struck. Backing without looking properly on the road test will probably result in a failing mark. Remember that we all will be called upon to take a driver's examination one day. Are *you* ready?

If you are unable to turn around to look back while backing, then don't back your vehicle! It is always easier to position or park your vehicle so that you are able to pull forward when starting.

Backing out of a driveway? Avoid this if at all possible. If unable to do so, then always back into the nearest lane, never back across other traffic lanes.

Miss your exit on the freeway? Don't back up! Many fatal crashes have resulted from freeway backing. Further, most all backing on any public roadway is illegal and can result in a reckless or careless driving citation. It would be better to drive to the next exit yourself than to be carried there by an ambulance!

INFAMOUS DRIVING BEHAVIOR NO. 6

FAILURE TO POSITION VEHICLE CORRECTLY FOR TURN

Although Notorious Behavior No. 3, *"Turning From The Wrong Lane"* is very closely related to this one, these kinds of crashes usually result from drivers making a last minute decision to turn. Oftentimes more than one behavior is involved in a collision, and it is that combination of more than one driving error that proves to be expensive in terms of injuries and property damage.

The frequency of incidents involving pedestrians at intersections is another reason for highlighting this behavior. Unfortunately, pedestrians are often the victims of drivers who are maneuvering in an intersection and are out of position or turning from a wrong lane.

Last minute decisions are usually the result of not making "destination planning" a part of the driving process. In other words thinking, "Where am I going and how do I get there?" When we are unsure of our destination or exactly how to get there, we are probably more than likely going to make a wrong decision and not be in the proper position to make our turn. This brings us to the need for **position signaling**. What is that?

Position signaling is defined as, **"Communicating to others what your intentions are by your position on the roadway."** This kind of communication is in conjunction with, and in addition to, turning your signal on before you change lanes or make a turn.

Example: You know you are going to turn left two blocks ahead. By *"position signaling"* you begin positioning your vehicle on the roadway **before** you reach the intersection. This means you start to move your vehicle to the lane next to the centerline long before you reach the point where you intend to turn. (Probably at least the same distance as your signal for turning, or a minimum of 100 feet). Driver Examiners watch for this move!

The position signal has communicated to other drivers that you intend to make a turn from the correct position. This has not been "last minute" and will result in a smooth maneuver with no improper turn and no sudden decision that has forced another driver to make a move that compromised anyone's safety.

INFAMOUS DRIVING BEHAVIOR NO. 7

CHANGING LANES - NO SIGNAL

Again, impulse rears its ugly head. I personally do not know many senior drivers who are impulsive, but there is nothing that contributes to this kind of behavior except impulse. Failure to have developed the *"habit"* of signaling has resulted in many crashes.

We can *prevent* a crash by **never making a move on the roadway unless we have told others of our intentions, by signaling in advance of our lane change.**

Safe Driving Tip: Avoid being pre-occupied or distracted. This is a deadly killer. It may keep you from communicating with other drivers. Being aware of the causes of collisions due to lane changes will help you plan your drive, and eliminate impulsive last minute lane changes without a signal.

Don't swing away from a vehicle approaching your lane from a side street. True, some drivers rush up to the stop sign and you may feel they are not going to stop. But your sudden swing out of your lane would probably not save you from a crash anyway. The better part of valor is to stay in your lane while driving, preferably the right hand lane, and always signal your lane change.

Safe Driving Tip: Plan ahead! Anticipate your lane changes. Communicate your changes by positioning your vehicle correctly and signaling your intention early.

66

INFAMOUS DRIVING BEHAVIOR NO. 8

LANE STRADDLING

Straddling the **"lane lines,"** or driving in two lanes at the same time, is not only a bad habit but can *provoke* drivers behind you to make moves that can be dangerous to them and others. Why do drivers straddle lanes? Probably, because they feel more comfortable when avoiding parked cars or other traffic. The center of the road may be, at times, the most comfortable place to be.

Just as every street has a **"center line,"** whether marked or not, so too, every street or highway has "lane lines" that may or may not be marked. It is vital that we observe these lane lines, even if we have to *imagine* them as always being there.

When we are teaching drivers the importance of not straddling lane lines the example is always used of how to make a correct left turn. As we approach an intersection for a left turn we visually make sure where the center line is and move from the right hand lane over to the lane next to the center line, or the left hand lane of the right side of the street. This is the correct position to be in when we start to make our left turn. Here especially, we do not want to be "lane straddling" while waiting to make our left turn. **Remember to keep your front wheels straight so that if you are rear-ended you are not pushed left into oncoming traffic.**

In fact, correct lane positioning at this point will make the possibility of being struck in the rear more remote. Too many rear-end crashes result from drivers being in the wrong position on the road, in the wrong lane, or straddling two lanes. This is a bad habit you do not want to have!

If you have developed good driving habits, you will not have to think about where you are on the street now, or later, when you are taking your driver's test.

DRIVING TOO SLOWLY

This behavior is what causes other drivers to become noticeably upset at senior drivers. Some slow moving vehicles are required by law to display an orange triangle on the rear as a means of identification, and some younger drivers have said that they would like to see that orange triangle on some seniors' cars. While I am sure they are not serious, we should recognize the need to prevent collisions by not driving too slowly.

Vehicles traveling at normal safe speeds can be dangerously influenced by slow moving vehicles, and crashes many times result. When a slow moving driver causes others to take chances in order to pass a collision may occur, sometimes with fatal results. The safe driver knows that it is illegal to drive slower than the posted minimum speed *unless* a slow speed is necessary because of existing weather, traffic, or road conditions.

If you cannot keep up with the posted speeds on a two-lane road and vehicles are lined up behind you, it would be courteous and considerate to signal, pull onto the shoulder safely, and stop until the vehicles have passed.

Safe Driving Tip: Pay attention to traffic flow. Drive at the posted speed. Keep to the right.

DRIVING AFTER DRINKING

Almost everyone is aware of the dangers of driving after drinking. Alcohol consumption is a major factor in more than half of all driving fatalities each year (U.S. Department of Transportation). However, what is not so well known is that ***senior drivers achieve the same level of intoxication as younger persons after consuming fewer drinks***.

In addition, it is recognized that alcohol depresses and slows bodily functions and reflexes. Driving after consuming *just one drink* can significantly impair the ability of anyone, but especially a senior driver, to operate a vehicle safely. This is exactly what we do not want to happen. We do not want to have slower reactions that result in impaired abilities.

Under most state laws it is a crime to operate, drive, or be in physical control of a motor vehicle if one has an alcohol concentration level (ACL) *at or above from .08% to .10%.* Yet, in just one state, 26.5% of drivers killed or injured had an ACL above the legal level.

We feel that there is *no safe level* of alcohol consumption that will not impair performance. While this view is a personal one and not popular with some drivers, legislators or even judges, there is only one way to ensure that your ACL level does not impair your ability to drive. ***Do not drive after drinking!*** We are not saying that one cannot enjoy a social occasion where alcohol is served. But, if you do, make sure you have a sober designated driver!

Every vehicle should be driven by a sober driver!

WHAT HAVE I LEARNED?

TRUE OR FALSE?

1. Failure to yield the right-of-way is the cause of most ALL crashes.
2. We can always assume other drivers will give us the right-of-way.
3. Before we start forward on the green light we must look both ways.
4. It is all right to enter an intersection on the yellow light if we can speed up to clear the intersection.
5. Failure to stop for a red signal is becoming an epidemic, so we must be aware of the possibility that an aggressive driver may force us to avoid a crash even when we have the green light.
6. We do not have to stop before making a right turn on a red light.
7. A few seconds of inattention can put us in a dangerous situation.
8. If all drivers made turns from or into the proper lane, the chance of a crash would be minimized.
9. If we are involved in a preventable collision it may possibly raise our insurance rates.
10. It is acceptable to use only our mirrors when backing.
11. We only need to signal when we can see that someone is going to be affected by our lane change.
12. We can provoke other drivers to make dangerous moves if we straddle lanes or drive too slowly.
13. Seniors achieve the same levels of intoxication as younger persons when consuming fewer drinks.

ANSWERS

1. F
2. F
3. T
4. F
5. T
6. F
7. T
8. T
9. T
10. F
11. F
12. T
13. T

Chapter Seven

TRAFFIC SIGNS & MARKINGS

Some Key Points in this Chapter

- Revising standards for traffic signs and markings.

- 21st Century technology to make driving safer.

- Why be "aware," and the consequences of not taking advantage of help to be a safer driver.

- Seniors will improve their collision rates!

Chapter Seven

TRAFFIC SIGNS & MARKINGS - SOME OLD, SOME NEW

 Some of us found driving freedom on the road in the 30's and 40's when roadways were two lanes wide. Today we are driving on roadways that, in some places, have multiples of six and eight lanes going in each direction. What a change!

Because of age-related declining driving abilities by many senior drivers, federal and state traffic safety agencies are recognizing the need to revise standards in their manuals on Uniform Traffic Control Devices. As a part of the move towards greater uniformity and clarity in road signs, we have seen technology change signs that communicate by words to those that communicate by symbols that are instantly recognized by every driver.

As discussed earlier, when groups of senior drivers were asked to identify the meanings of newer signs, there were many seniors who were unable to recognize one or more of the new signs or interpret their meanings. How about you? How is *your* sign language? Signs, shapes of signs, and color coding should be a part of each driver's subconscious knowledge to bring about instinctive reaction.

All states are using the International Traffic Control Standards signs with the red & white *"Yield"* and *"Do Not Enter"* signs, along with the use of the red circle with diagonal slash to indicate a prohibited traffic movement. Also, all yellow/black warning signs now utilize directional arrows.

Can you identify these signs of our times?

Unless we become aware and learn about new signs and signals, we could possibly make a serious or even fatal mistake. Recently a senior driver admitted not recognizing a new red and white "Do Not Enter" sign posted on a freeway on ramp. After driving the wrong way, entering the freeway and driving against traffic, the driver struck another vehicle head-on, killing one and critically injuring another. Sad, yes, avoidable, yes! There was an immediate reaction among the driving public. "Get those older drivers off the road." "Make seniors pass a test before they can drive." More fuel added to the fires already burning in state lawmakers' offices among those advocating senior road testing.

Safe Driving Tip: Contact your Motor Vehicle Department, Safety Division, or office where you renew your driver's license and obtain a personal copy of the State Driver's Manual. Bring yourself up to date on the newest traffic signs, signals and markings. (See Appendix for the address list of Driver License Administrators).

Significant improvements are being made in driving safety, more will be made, and seniors can and will improve their collision rates, even with more vehicles on the road and more seniors driving. While many of the improvements being made are clearly aimed at senior drivers, all drivers benefit and like the changes. And even though these changes are costly, the change is inevitable, as 75 million baby boomers now in their 50's are approaching retirement. Think of it! By 2010, 17% of those old enough to drive will be 65 years of age or older, and that will rise to 25% in 2030!

Our driving independence is important to all of us seniors, as we need to keep up with the social and economic aspects of our society. In the future we will see still more 21st Century technology to make driving safer:
1. *Infra-Red Sensors* built into the windshields of vehicles to help drivers spot signs and/or obstacles along dark roads.
2. *Heads-Up Displays* to let drivers look straight ahead and see vehicle information, speed, etc. displayed on the windshield glass.
3. *Rear View Mirrors* that automatically compensate for bright lights.
4. *Global Positioning Systems* computerized dashboard map displays that utilize global positioning (GPS) to tell drivers where they are at all times.
5. *Collision Avoidance Systems* will use radar to alert drivers to objects in their blind spots or even approaching from the side or front.
6. *Night-Vision* heat sensitive systems that detect objects in the dark as far away as 500 yards, projecting them on a windshield display.

Don't hang up your keys! Keep your wheels! Keep up to date on new signs and signals! Learn the new sign language!

WHAT HAVE I LEARNED?

TRUE OR FALSE?

1. Traffic safety agencies are making changes in signs, signals and markings to accommodate senior drivers.
2. Driving will be made safer by the technological advances being made in vehicle design.
3. Not recognizing signs or signals could result in a fatal crash.
4. We can contact our state Motor Vehicle Administrator for up to date information on signs, signals and roadway markings.
5. Our driving independence is really not all that important to society as a whole.

ANSWERS

    1. T
    2. T
    3. T
    4. T
    5. F

Chapter Eight

SAFE WALKING TIPS FOR PEDESTRIANS

Some Key Points in this Chapter

- We could be walking more safely!

- Walking defensively.

- Cross streets only at intersections.

- How to be "seen" when walking.

Chapter Eight

SAFE WALKING TIPS FOR PEDESTRIANS

LET'S WALK SAFELY TOO

For statistical purposes, any crash where a pedestrian is struck and injured is defined as a pedestrian crash, and this makes good sense. In 1997, there were 1,419 crashes in which a pedestrian was killed or injured by a motor vehicle. About 4% of pedestrian crashes resulted in death, compared to about ½ of 1% of all crashes, so there is reason to be concerned. We could be walking more safely!

Pedestrians who were crossing a roadway or street were by far the ones most involved in these kinds of crashes. One hundred fifty-nine of the 1,419 pedestrians injured or killed were seniors, age 55 years or over. Obviously, there is need to improve this picture. How can we do it? Just as we talked earlier about driving our vehicles defensively we must do certain things to **walk defensively**.

Safety Tip: **Always** walk *facing* traffic and as far to the left as possible. As I sit here at my computer writing this chapter, I can observe people walking by on the street with their backs to traffic, and most of them are seniors.

All of us must cross streets, perhaps after we have parked our vehicle. When you do, **cross only at the intersection and obey the signals**. Never jaywalk, and never start crossing between parked cars. You cannot see an approaching car and they cannot see you. The intersection corner is the safest place to cross and many of them are well marked. That is where drivers expect to see a pedestrian crossing the street.

The majority of pedestrian crashes occur after 3 p.m. and into the dusk and evening hours, so **wear light colored clothing**. **Reflective clothing or strips** for attachment to our clothing are available at sports stores.

Drivers with *"safety awareness"* will carry this over to those times they must be pedestrians, and *walk defensively*!

WHAT HAVE I LEARNED?

TRUE OR FALSE?

1. Always walk facing traffic and as far to the left as possible.
2. Cross the street at an intersection because that is where other drivers expect to see you.
3. Most all pedestrian crashes occur between 11 a.m. and 1 p.m.
4. Everyone should walk defensively.

ANSWERS

1. T
2. T
3. F
4. T

IN CLOSING

The germ of ideas which form the basis for this Senior Driver's Guide stem from many years of experience in the driver safety field, along with my analysis of the crash-causing factors associated with senior crashes. My goal has been to provide enough detailed information to enable **any driver** to survive in the challenging driving environment we find ourselves in today.

When we drive, most of us are reminded in one way or another of our deteriorating skill levels associated with aging, and so have taken some corrective steps on our own. But there is still more we can and must do!

This "How To" guidebook, with its safe driving tips and techniques, provides key information needed to enable the concerned reader to correct some bad habits, make appropriate changes in how they drive, and make themselves smarter, safer, senior drivers. In fact one reader said, "I now feel that when the day comes that I am asked to take that road test, I know I'll pass it!" Some readers have said they were inspired to correct some habits that they had not realized could be detrimental to their safety.

Another reader added that he did not realize there was so much he did not know about driving, and was pleased with the detail and basic review, especially the crash prevention tips.

Perhaps for some readers, the detail may seem to be too much to remember. But you will not regret the time you spend reading this, nor the effort you make to put into practice the safe driving tips we have put in the spotlight - especially for you!

Have a safe trip! Enjoy your driving!

DRIVER LICENSE ADMINISTRATORS
These offices will furnish Driver's Manuals

ALABAMA
Driver License Div.
Dept. of Public Safety
500 Dexter Ave.
P.O.Box 1471
Montgomery, AL 36102
(334) 242-4240

ALASKA
Div. of Motor Vehicles
Dept. of Administration
5700 E. Tudor Rd.
Anchorage, AK 99507
(907) 269-5559

ARIZONA
Motor Vehicle Div.
Dept. of Transportation
1801 W. Jefferson
Phoenix, AZ 85007
)602) 255-8152

ARKANSAS
Dept. of Administration
P.O.Box 1272
Little Rock, AR 72203
(501) 682-7000

CALIFORNIA
Dept. of Motor Vehicles
P.O.Box 932328
Sacramento, CA 94232
(916) 657-7061

COLORADO
Dept. of Revenue
Denver, CO 80261
(303) 572-5653

CONNECTICUT
Dept. of Motor Vehicles
60 State St.
Wethersfield, CT 06109
(860) 566-2240

DELAWARE
Div. of Motor Vehicles
Dept. of Public Safety
P.O.Box 698
Dover, DE 19903
(302) 739-4421

DIST. OF COLUMBIA
Transportation Systems
Dept. of Public Works
65 K Street NE
Washington, DC 20002
(202) 727-1735

FLORIDA
Hwy. Safety & Motor Veh.
2900 Apalachee Pkwy.
Tallahassee, FL 32399
(850)488-4597

GEORGIA
Motor Vehicle Division
270 Washington St. SW
Atlanta, GA 30303
(404) 656-4156

IDAHO
Dept. of Transportation
P.O.Box 7129
Boise, ID 83707-1129
(208) 334-8606

ILLINOIS
Secretary of State
213 State House
Springfield, IL 62756
(217) 782-2201

INDIANA
Bur.of Motor Vehicles
IGC North, Room 440
Indianapolis, IN 46204
(317) 233-2349

IOWA
Dept. of Transportation
P.O.Box 10382
Des Moines, IA 50306
(515) 237-3202

KANSAS
Dept. of Motor Vehicles
Docking State Office Bldg.
915 Harrison
Topeka, KS 66612
(785) 296-3601

KENTUCKY
Dept. of Vehicle Regulation
State Office Bldg.
501 High Street
Frankfort, KY 40601
(502) 564-7000

LOUISIANA
Public Safety Dept.
P.O.Box 66614
Baton Rouge, LA 70896
(504) 925-6335

MAINE
Division of Motor Vehicles
Department of State
29 State House Station
Augusta, ME 04333
(207) 287-2761

MARYLAND
Dept. of Transportation
6601 Ritchie Hwy., NE
Glen Burnie, MD 21062
(410) 768-7274

MASSACHUSETTS
Registry of Motor Vehicles
1135 Tremont Street
Boston, MA 02120-2103
(617) 351-2700

MICHIGAN
Service Delivery Admin.
Dept. of State
7064 Crowner Dr.
Lansing, MI 48918
(517) 322-1528

MINNESOTA
Driver & Vehicle Services
Dept. of Public Safety
445 Minnesota Street
Saint Paul. MN 55101-5195

MISSISSIPPI
Motor Vehicle Commission
1755 Leilia Drive, Ste. 200
P.O.Box 16873
Jackson, MS 39236
(601) 987-3995

MISSOURI
Div. of Driver Licenses
Dept. of Revenue
P.O.Box 629
Jefferson City, MO 65105
(573) 751-4429

NEBRASKA
Dept. of Motor Vehicles
P.O.Box 94789
Lincoln, NE 68509-4789
(402) 471-9594

NEVADA
Dept. of Public Safety
55 Wright Way
Carson City, NV 89711-0900
(702) 687-5375

NEW HAMPSHIRE
Div. of Motor Vehicles
Department of Safety
10 Hazen Drive
Concord, NH 03305-0002
(603) 271-2484

NEW JERSEY
Div. of Motor Vehicle Svs.
Dept. of Law & Public Safety
225 E. State Street
P.O.Box 160
Trenton, NJ 08625-0160
(609) 292-7500

NEW MEXICO
Motor Vehicle Division
P.O.Box 1028
Santa Fe, NM 87504-1028
(505) 827-2294

NEW YORK
Dept. of Motor Vehicles
Swan Street Bldg.
Empire State Plaza
Albany, NY 12228
(518) 474-0841

NORTH CAROLINA
Dept. of Transportation
1100 New Bern Avenue
Raleigh, NC 27697-000
(919) 733-2403

NORTH DAKOTA
Driver/Vehicle Services
Dept. of Transportation
608 E. Blvd. Ave.
Bismarck, ND 58505-0700
(701) 328-2581

OHIO
Department of Public Safety
4300 Kimberly Parkway
Columbus, OH 752-7500
(614) 752-7500

OKLAHOMA
Motor Vehicle Division
4334 NW Expy., Ste. 183
Oklahoma City, OK 73116
(405) 521-2375

OREGON
Dept. of Transportation
1905 Lana Ave., NE
Salem, OR 97314
(503) 945-5100

PENNSYLVANIA
Dept. of Transportation
1101 So. Front St.
Harrisburg, PA 17104
(717) 787-2304

RHODE ISLAND
Div. of Motor Vehicles
286 Main Street
Pawtucket, RI 02860
(401) 222-2970

SOUTH CAROLINA
Dept. of Public Safety
5410 Broad River Rd.
Columbia, SC 29210
(803) 896-7839

SOUTH DAKOTA
Div. of Drivers Licensing
Public Safety Building
118 W. Capitol Avenue
Pierre, SD 57501
(605) 773-5949

TENNESSEE
Department of Safety
1283 Airways Plaza
Nashville, TN 37243
(615) 741-3101

TEXAS
Dept. of Transportation
Motor Vehicle Division
200 E. Riverside Drive
Building 150
Austin, TX 78704
(512) 416-4800

UTAH
Tax Commission
210 North 1950 W.
Salt Lake City, UT84134
(801) 297-3500

VERMONT
Dept. of Motor Vehicles
Agency of Transportation
133 State Street
Montpelier, VT 05602
(802) 828-2011

VIRGINIA
Dept. of Motor Vehicles
2300 W. Broad St.
Richmond, VA 23220
(804) 367-6606

WASHINGTON
Vehicle Services
Dept. of Licensing
P.O.Box 48020
Olympia, WA 98507
(360) 902-3818

WEST VIRGINIA
Dept. of Transportation
Bldg. 3, Rm. 337
1900 Kanawha Blvd. E
Charleston, WV 25305
(304) 558-2723

WISCONSIN
Dept. of Transportation
4802 Sheboygan Av.
P.O.Box 7949
Madison, WI 53707
(608) 266-2233

WYOMING
Dept. of Revenue & Taxation
122 W 25th Street
Cheyenne, WY 82002
(307) 777-5216

Index

A

B

C

D

E

F

G

H

I

L

M

N

- National Highway Transportation Safety Administration-
  - NHTSA, fault in crashes, **5**
  - injury, **43**
- National Institute on Aging, research, **3**
- No. 1 traffic violation for seniors, **19**

O

- Other driver, the bad guy, **33**

P

- Parking, high risk, **39**
  - illegal, **39**
- Passing, on right, when permitted, **37**
  - trucks, **38**
  - when not to, **37**
- Pay attention or pay, **55**
- Position signaling, **38, 63**

R

- Rate yourself, a checklist, **8**
- Reaction time, **23, 24**
- Red light, crashes, 1/4 million, **53**
  - complete stop, **53**
  - rules, **54**
  - Safe Driving Tip, **59**
- Retain your license and independence, **33**
- Right-of-way, failure to yield, **19**
  - left turners, **57**
  - rules, **34, 35, 54**
  - when to yield, **34**
- Right on red, **35**
  - the "right", **35**
  - when allowed, statute, **53**
- Right turn, **57**
- Running red lights, **53**
  - cameras at intersections, **53**

U

V

W

Y

Bibliography

Emergency Medical Services Techniques and Applications, Federal Emergency Management Agency, United States Fire Administration, Emmitsburg, MD 21727.

Insurance Institute for Highway Safety, 1005 N. Glebe Road, Arlington, VA 22201.

Manual on Uniform Traffic Control Devices, U.S. Department of Transportation, Federal Highway Administration, Washington, D.C. 20590.

Minnesota Driver's Manual, Minnesota Department of Public Safety, 444 Cedar Street, Saint Paul, MN 55101.

Minnesota Motor Vehicle Crash Facts, Minnesota Department of Public Safety, Office of Traffic Safety, 444 Cedar Street, Saint Paul, MN 55101.

Model Safe Driving Guidelines, Occupational Safety & Health Administration (OSHA) Guidelines for Ambulance Providers, Federal Office of OSHA, Washington, D.C. 20590.

National Highway Traffic Safety Administration Facts (NHTSA), U.S. Department of Transportation, Washington, D.C. 20590.

National Institute on Aging - Various Studies, 600 Maryland Avenue, S.W. Wing 100, Washington, D.C. 20024.

Senior Driver Facts, California Department of Motor Vehicles, P.O. Box 932328 Sacramento, CA 94232.

Spotlight on Safety, Compilations, and Derivative Works by Ken D. Smith, Canary Publications, P.O. Box 28871, Oakdale, MN 55128.

Traffic Safety For Older Persons, The National Highway Traffic Safety Administration, U.S., Department of Transportation, National Highway Traffic Safety Administration, Washington, D.C. 20590.

ABOUT THE AUTHOR

Ken D. Smith is a graduate of Northwestern Traffic Institute, Northwestern University, Evanston, IL, Police Traffic Records. His years within the Minnesota Department of Public Safety started in the early 1950's as Driver License Examiner. He assisted in the design, development and implementation of the Driver Improvement Evaluation program with subsequent appointment as Supervisor of the Accident Records Department. During his tenure he developed various programs for accident statistical analysis and driver-vehicle analysis for publication. He also developed systems, forms and methods for utilization of crash investigation data into the State safety program

His experience includes instructing various law enforcement agencies in traffic accident analysis and records, i.e. Minnesota Highway Patrol Staff Command Schools, Police Officers Training Schools and the Suburban Police Training Academy. He designed curriculum and conducted the Safe Driving School for Ramsey County Juvenile Court and also the Adult Driver Education program for the City of Saint Paul, Minnesota.

He has been a member of the National Safety Council Accident Records training program for Cities, and Contributing member of the National Committee on Uniform Motor Vehicle Accident Classification Codes.

He designed and implemented the Minnesota Department of Transportation approved Defensive Driver Training Course for Special Transportation Drivers. Further, he was the originator and operator of the first "behind-the-wheel" driver training school in the City of Saint Paul, Minnesota.

He has authored various driver safety instruction manuals and other works:

EMS Fleet Risk Management, A data base program.
Driver Safety Program for EMS Drivers.
Vehicle Safety Review Committee Manual.
Motor Vehicle Traffic Accident Investigators Manual.
Manual for Classification of Preventable/ Non Preventable
     Motor Vehicle Crashes.
Minnesota Motor Vehicle Accident Report.
Police Traffic Accident Report.
Driver Handbook for Emergency Vehicle Operators.
Guidelines and Selection Profiles for the Driver Hiring Process.
Vehicle Safety Review Committee Guidelines, a Manual.
Guidebook for Determining Preventability of Vehicle Crashes.

He last served as Safety Coordinator for Health Span Transportation Services, a division of Allina Health System. In his capacity as Safety Coordinator, he developed and implemented a Driver Safety Program for Fleet Drivers.

Since his retirement, he acts as consultant for the Vehicle Crash Review Committee for Health Span Transportation Services. He also frequently authors Driver Safety news articles in the Stillwater Gazette, Stillwater, Minnesota.

HOW DOES AGE AFFECT OUR DRIVING?

RATE YOURSELF: A "BEFORE YOU DRIVE" CHECKLIST

Indicate Yes or No   **(Refer back to Chapter 2 for answers)**

_____ 1. Have you on occasion missed a sign or signal?

_____ 2. Are other drivers in too big of a rush?

_____ 3. Are gaps in traffic harder to judge?

_____ 4. Roads are getting confusing or I sometimes get lost?

_____ 5. Cars suddenly come from nowhere?

_____ 6. Do you take any medicine that may impair your driving?

_____ 7. Is it getting difficult to make a sharp turn?

_____ 8. Do drivers seem to stop suddenly in front of you?

_____ 9. Is highway and freeway driving getting to be difficult?

_____ 10. Night driving is sometimes hard to cope with.

_____ 11. I always wear my seat belt.

_____ 12. I lose my temper at some traffic situations.

_____ 13. I shy away from turning left at some intersections.

_____ 14. Usually I drive with one foot on the brake and one on the gas.

_____ 15. I always use my turn signal when turning, changing lanes and driving away from the curb.

_____ 16. Have you gotten a citation for a moving violation or a warning from a traffic officer ?

_____ 17. I have had more than one minor vehicle crash during the past two years.

_____ 18. I often watch scenery and talk to others while driving.

HOW DOES AGE AFFECT OUR DRIVING?

RATE YOURSELF: A "BEFORE YOU DRIVE" CHECKLIST

Indicate Yes or No   (Refer back to Chapter 2 for answers)

_____ 1. Have you on occasion missed a sign or signal?

_____ 2. Are other drivers in too big of a rush?

_____ 3. Are gaps in traffic harder to judge?

_____ 4. Roads are getting confusing or I sometimes get lost?

_____ 5. Cars suddenly come from nowhere?

_____ 6. Do you take any medicine that may impair your driving?

_____ 7. Is it getting difficult to make a sharp turn?

_____ 8. Do drivers seem to stop suddenly in front of you?

_____ 9. Is highway and freeway driving getting to be difficult?

_____ 10. Night driving is sometimes hard to cope with.

_____ 11. I always wear my seat belt.

_____ 12. I lose my temper at some traffic situations.

_____ 13. I shy away from turning left at some intersections.

_____ 14. Usually I drive with one foot on the brake and one on the gas.

_____ 15. I always use my turn signal when turning, changing lanes and driving away from the curb.

_____ 16. Have you gotten a citation for a moving violation or a warning from a traffic officer ?

_____ 17. I have had more than one minor vehicle crash during the past two years.

_____ 18. I often watch scenery and talk to others while driving.

HOW DOES AGE AFFECT OUR DRIVING?

RATE YOURSELF: A "BEFORE YOU DRIVE" CHECKLIST

Indicate Yes or No   (Refer back to Chapter 2 for answers)

_____ 1. Have you on occasion missed a sign or signal?

_____ 2. Are other drivers in too big of a rush?

_____ 3. Are gaps in traffic harder to judge?

_____ 4. Roads are getting confusing or I sometimes get lost?

_____ 5. Cars suddenly come from nowhere?

_____ 6. Do you take any medicine that may impair your driving?

_____ 7. Is it getting difficult to make a sharp turn?

_____ 8. Do drivers seem to stop suddenly in front of you?

_____ 9. Is highway and freeway driving getting to be difficult?

_____ 10. Night driving is sometimes hard to cope with.

_____ 11. I always wear my seat belt.

_____ 12. I lose my temper at some traffic situations.

_____ 13. I shy away from turning left at some intersections.

_____ 14. Usually I drive with one foot on the brake and one on the gas.

_____ 15. I always use my turn signal when turning, changing lanes and driving away from the curb.

_____ 16. Have you gotten a citation for a moving violation or a warning from a traffic officer ?

_____ 17. I have had more than one minor vehicle crash during the past two years.

_____ 18. I often watch scenery and talk to others while driving.

104

HOW DOES AGE AFFECT OUR DRIVING?

RATE YOURSELF: A "BEFORE YOU DRIVE" CHECKLIST

Indicate Yes or No   (Refer back to Chapter 2 for answers)

_____ 1. Have you on occasion missed a sign or signal?

_____ 2. Are other drivers in too big of a rush?

_____ 3. Are gaps in traffic harder to judge?

_____ 4. Roads are getting confusing or I sometimes get lost?

_____ 5. Cars suddenly come from nowhere?

_____ 6. Do you take any medicine that may impair your driving?

_____ 7. Is it getting difficult to make a sharp turn?

_____ 8. Do drivers seem to stop suddenly in front of you?

_____ 9. Is highway and freeway driving getting to be difficult?

_____ 10. Night driving is sometimes hard to cope with.

_____ 11. I always wear my seat belt.

_____ 12. I lose my temper at some traffic situations.

_____ 13. I shy away from turning left at some intersections.

_____ 14. Usually I drive with one foot on the brake and one on the gas.

_____ 15. I always use my turn signal when turning, changing lanes and driving away from the curb.

_____ 16. Have you gotten a citation for a moving violation or a warning from a traffic officer ?

_____ 17. I have had more than one minor vehicle crash during the past two years.

_____ 18. I often watch scenery and talk to others while driving.

THE SENIOR DRIVER'S GUIDEBOOK

HOW TO KEEP DRIVING LONGER

AND SURVIVE IN THE

21st CENTURY

This guidebook provides the framework for developing the skills needed to cope in a dangerous and rapidly changing driving environment.

A collection of 100's of Safe Driving Tips and strategies as a refresher to improve driving performance and help drivers pass any driving test they may be required to take.

Send your check and the coupon below to:

Five Star Publishing
P. O. Box 4
Stillwater, MN 55082-4298

For addition information or to order, call: 612-362-5966
Copyright © 1999 by Ken D. Smith.

Rush my personal copy of the book, **The Seniors Driver's Guidebook - How To Keep Driving Longer And Survive In The 21st Century** now.

Please send ___ copy(s) at $24.95 each postage paid. Enclosed is check or money order for $_____ no cash or C.O.D.'s. To order by phone, call toll free: 1-888-769-7751, Ext. 2001. Copyright © **1999 by Ken D. Smith.**

_____ Charge to my: _____ *VISA   _____ *Mastercard   _____ *Discover

Card #: _____ Expiration Date: _____

Signature: _____

Name: (Please print.) _____

Address: _____Phone (   )_____

City _____ State _____ Zip _____

*For Visa/Mastercard & Discover Card orders – Please call toll free at 1-888-769-7751 Ext.2001
Please allow 4-6 weeks for delivery.
If not completely satisfied, return within thirty (30) days for full refund.

THE SENIOR DRIVER'S GUIDEBOOK

HOW TO KEEP DRIVING LONGER

AND SURVIVE IN THE

21st CENTURY

This guidebook provides the framework for developing the skills needed to cope in a dangerous and rapidly changing driving environment.

A collection of 100's of Safe Driving Tips and strategies as a refresher to improve driving performance and help drivers pass any driving test they may be required to take.

Send your check and the coupon below to:

Five Star Publishing
P. O. Box 4
Stillwater, MN 55082-4298

For addition information or to order, call: 612-362-5966
Copyright © 1999 by Ken D. Smith.

Rush my personal copy of the book, **The Seniors Driver's Guidebook - How To Keep Driving Longer And Survive In The 21st Century** now.

Please send ___ copy(s) at $24.95 each postage paid. Enclosed is check or money order for $_____ no cash or C.O.D.'s. To order by phone, call toll free: 1-888-769-7751, Ext. 2001. Copyright © **1999 by Ken D. Smith.**

_____ Charge to my: _____ *VISA _____ *Mastercard _____ *Discover

Card #: _____ Expiration Date: _____

Signature: _____

Name: (Please print.) _____

Address: _____Phone (   )_____

City _____ State _____ Zip _____

*For Visa/Mastercard & Discover Card orders – Please call toll free at 1-888-769-7751 Ext.2001
Please allow 4-6 weeks for delivery.
If not completely satisfied, return within thirty (30) days for full refund.

THE SENIOR DRIVER'S GUIDEBOOK

HOW TO KEEP DRIVING LONGER

AND SURVIVE IN THE

21st CENTURY

This guidebook provides the framework for developing the skills needed to cope in a dangerous and rapidly changing driving environment.

A collection of 100's of Safe Driving Tips and strategies as a refresher to improve driving performance and help drivers pass any driving test they may be required to take.

Send your check and the coupon below to:

Five Star Publishing
P. O. Box 4
Stillwater, MN 55082-4298

For addition information or to order, call: 612-362-5966
Copyright © 1999 by Ken D. Smith.

Rush my personal copy of the book, **The Seniors Driver's Guidebook - How To Keep Driving Longer And Survive In The 21st Century** now.

Please send ___ copy(s) at $24.95 each postage paid. Enclosed is check or money order for $_____ no cash or C.O.D.'s. To order by phone, call toll free: 1-888-769-7751, Ext. 2001. Copyright © **1999 by Ken D. Smith.**

_____ Charge to my: _____ *VISA _____ *Mastercard _____ *Discover

Card #: _____ Expiration Date: _____

Signature: _____

Name: (Please print.) _____

Address: _____ Phone ( )_____

City _____ State _____ Zip _____

*For Visa/Mastercard & Discover Card orders – Please call toll free at 1-888-769-7751 Ext.2001
Please allow 4-6 weeks for delivery.
If not completely satisfied, return within thirty (30) days for full refund.

THE SENIOR DRIVER'S GUIDEBOOK

HOW TO KEEP DRIVING LONGER

AND SURVIVE IN THE

21st CENTURY

This guidebook provides the framework for developing the skills needed to cope in a dangerous and rapidly changing driving environment.

A collection of 100's of Safe Driving Tips and strategies as a refresher to improve driving performance and help drivers pass any driving test they may be required to take.

Send your check and the coupon below to:

Five Star Publishing
P. O. Box 4
Stillwater, MN 55082-4298

For addition information or to order, call: 612-362-5966
Copyright © 1999 by Ken D. Smith.

Rush my personal copy of the book, **The Seniors Driver's Guidebook - How To Keep Driving Longer And Survive In The 21st Century** now.

Please send ___ copy(s) at $24.95 each postage paid. Enclosed is check or money order for $_____ no cash or C.O.D.'s. To order by phone, call toll free: 1-888-769-7751, Ext. 2001. Copyright © **1999 by Ken D. Smith.**

_____ Charge to my: _____ *VISA   _____ *Mastercard   _____ *Discover

Card #: _____ Expiration Date: _____

Signature: _____

Name: (Please print.) _____

Address: _____Phone (   )_____

City _____ State _____ Zip _____

*For Visa/Mastercard & Discover Card orders – Please call toll free at 1-888-769-7751 Ext.2001
Please allow 4-6 weeks for delivery.
If not completely satisfied, return within thirty (30) days for full refund.